Elegant Perfection

Masterpieces of Courtly and Religious Art from the Tokyo National Museum

Tokyo National Museum

The Museum of Fine Arts, Houston
Distributed by Yale University Press, New Haven and London

This catalogue was published to coincide with the opening of the Arts of Japan Gallery and the inaugural exhibition *Elegant Perfection: Masterpieces of Courtly and Religious Art from the Tokyo National Museum* at the Museum of Fine Arts, Houston, February 17 to April 8, 2012.

Distributed by Yale University Press, New Haven and London
www.yalebooks.com/art

Library of Congress Cataloging-in-Publication Data
Elegant perfection : masterpieces of courtly and religious art from the Tokyo National Museum / Tokyo National Museum.
p. cm.
Published to coincide with an exhibition held at the Museum of Fine Arts, Houston, Houston, Tex., Feb. 17-April 8, 2012.
Summary: "Twenty-six exquisite works of art from the esteemed collection of the Tokyo National Museum trace the religious and cultural history of Japan from ancient times through the nineteenth century" –Provided by publisher.
ISBN 978-0-300-17593-6 (hardcover)
1. Art, Japanese–Exhibitions.
2. Buddhist art–Japan–Exhibitions.
3. Art–Japan–Tokyo–Exhibitions.
4. Tokyo Kokuritsu Hakubutsukan–Exhibitions.
I. McCormick, Melissa, 1967-
II. Museum of Fine Arts, Houston.
N3750.T63A54 2011
709.52'07452135–dc22
2011009045

MFAH Publications Director
Diane Lovejoy

Edited by
Heather Brand

Designed by
Rigsby Hull

Translations by
Maiko Behr

Translations reviewed by
Tokyo National Museum
International Relations Section

All images courtesy
TNM Image Archives
Source: http://TnmArchives.jp/

Tokyo National Museum
Asami Ryūsuke (A.R.)
Curator of Japanese Sculpture

Furuya Takeshi (F.T.)
Curator of Japanese Archaeology

Imai Atsushi (I.A.)
Senior Curator of Asian Ceramics

Itō Shinji (I.S.)
Curator of Japanese Decorative Arts

Matsumoto Nobuyuki (M.N.)
Director of Curatorial Planning

Seya Ai (S.A.)
Assistant Curator of Japanese Painting

Shimatani Hiroyuki (S.H.)
Vice Executive Director

Shinagawa Yoshiya (S.Y.)
Assistant Curator of
Japanese Archaeology

Takeuchi Namiko (T.N.)
Curator of Japanese Decorative Arts

Yokoyama Azusa (Y.A.)
Assistant Curator of
Japanese Ceramics

with
Melissa McCormick
Professor of Japanese Art and Culture
Harvard University

and
Christine Starkman
Curator of Asian Art, Ancient to Contemporary
The Museum of Fine Arts, Houston

The Arts of Japan Gallery at the Museum of Fine Arts, Houston, is made possible with generous support from:

Japan Business Association of Houston 2011*
in memory of Mr. Seigo Arai

Nanako and Dale Tingleaf

Mitsui & Company (U.S.A.), Inc.

Penny and Paul Loyd

Mitsubishi Corporation

Sumitomo Corporation of America

GE Energy

Donna Fujimoto Cole

Drs. Ellin and Robert Grossman

Gulf States Toyota, Inc.

Mitsubishi International Corporation–Houston Branch

Akemi and Yasuhiko Saitoh

Miwa S. Sakashita and John R. Stroehlein

Satake USA Inc.

Taeko and Nobuya Tomita

Toshiba International Corporation

Nozomi and Ryuji Watanabe

*Japan Business Association of Houston 2011
gift made possible in part by:

JX Group

Kaneka Texas Corporation

Kuraray America, Inc.

Mitsubishi Caterpillar Forklift America, Inc.

NOLTEX LLC

Toshiba International Corporation

Contributors as of publication date.

Contents

Forewords

It is a great pleasure to extend my heartfelt congratulations on the opening of the newly dedicated Arts of Japan Gallery at the Museum of Fine Arts, Houston.

The Tokyo National Museum was established in 1872 and is the largest museum in Japan, with a collection currently totaling about 113,000 items and a site comprising six exhibition gallery buildings and a Research and Information Center. The museum's activities focus on acquisitions, preservation, research, exhibitions, and dissemination of its collections, which consist of cultural properties primarily from Japan and surrounding Asian countries. We welcome more than one million visitors annually, of which approximately 10 percent are visitors from abroad. As a result, contributing to awareness of Japanese cultural arts overseas is of profound importance to us.

With the inaugural exhibition *Elegant Perfection: Masterpieces of Courtly and Religious Art from the Tokyo National Museum*, we welcome you to enjoy a selection of superb examples of Japanese aristocratic and Buddhist art that reflect an aesthetic tradition that can be traced back to ancient times, including the National Treasure *Man'yōshū*, vol. 9 (Takamatsunomiya version), a masterwork of calligraphy.

Many Japanese art objects, such as certain paintings and textiles, cannot be exhibited for extended periods for conservation reasons due to the fragility of their materials. For this Arts of Japan Gallery, we have selected a number of ceramics, metalworks, and other objects that can endure prolonged exposure, and are pleased to offer them for a two-year loan period. This is the first time a group of works from the Tokyo National Museum collection will be exhibited for such an extended period in the United States.

We hope that by providing visitors an opportunity for firsthand experience of Japanese art, the Arts of Japan Gallery at the Museum of Fine Arts, Houston, will deepen understanding of Japanese culture abroad and become a new center of cultural exchange between Japan and the United States.

Zeniya Masami
Executive Director
Tokyo National Museum

Japanese culture goes back more than five thousand years. Yet despite its origins in antiquity, Japan is a nation of the future. This duality of yesterday and tomorrow is what makes Japan a unique place in the world. In Japan, ancient landmarks stand tranquilly among imposing skyscrapers. Early customs continue to take place against the backdrop of the world's most advanced technologies. With one of the largest and most powerful economies in the world, and as a center of international activity, Japan has been able to embrace its traditions while finding its place in the larger global, political, diplomatic, and economic arenas.

Japan's complex identity is reflected in the diverse works chosen for display in the new Arts of Japan Gallery at the Museum of Fine Arts, Houston (MFAH). The works in the gallery range from Neolithic to contemporary art, demonstrating the rich culture of Japan across generations. Through the Portal Project, a contemporary artist will create a site-specific installation that will stand beside both modern and ancient masterpieces. The gallery will thus be a reflection of Japan's dynamic and multifaceted character.

Over the past thirty years, the MFAH's collection of Japanese art has continued to increase with the addition of such important works as a figure of the Amida Buddha and a *haniwa* warrior. As the museum's holdings have grown, so have its local and international relationships. The MFAH's partnership with the Tokyo National Museum will bring national treasures to Houston. These objects will illuminate visitors with the beauty and artistry of Japan's ancient culture. We are so pleased to be working with the Tokyo National Museum to show visitors Japan's remarkable creative heritage. Through the new Arts of Japan Gallery, the MFAH will be able to showcase Japan's vast legacy for generations to come. We extend special thanks to our friends and colleagues from all over the world who have generously given so much to make this goal a reality.

Gwendolyn H. Goffe
Interim Director
The Museum of Fine Arts, Houston

Acknowledgments

The Arts of Japan Gallery project at the Museum of Fine Arts, Houston, would not have been possible had not many people from all over the world generously given their amazing support and efforts to every stage from its conception to its grand opening. My sincere gratitude goes to Zeniya Masami, executive director, Matsumoto Nobuyuki, director of curatorial planning, and Shimatani Hiroyuki, vice executive director, of the Tokyo National Museum (TNM) for their enthusiasm and unwavering support of the magnificent loans from the museum's stellar collection to the Arts of Japan Gallery at the MFAH.

I would like to extend special thanks to the Honorable Takahiko Watabe, deputy-consul general of Japan in Houston, and the Honorable Tsutomu Osawa, the previous consul general of Japan in Houston, for their great help and joint efforts in sharing Japanese culture with the larger Houston community. My sincerest gratitude also goes to the Japanese Business Association of Houston and its 2011 president, Mr. Shinichiro Akiba, and vice president, Mr. Ryuji Watanabe, for their constant assistance in this important project, and for generously offering the MFAH their many resources in the local Japanese community and abroad to help ensure the success of the Arts of Japan Gallery. My heartfelt thanks also go to Dr. Marjorie Horning, Dr. and Mrs. James Butler, Stephen Hamilton, and Dale and Nanako Tingleaf for helping to initiate the creation of a substantial program of Japanese art at the MFAH and for facilitating initial contact with cultural and artistic institutions in Japan.

I would also like to thank Emura Tomoko, art historian and researcher at the National Research Institute for Cultural Properties, Tokyo, for helping us to establish initial contacts with the Tokyo National Museum. The staff at the TNM has been of tremendous and invaluable help managing the loans and arranging for the objects' safe arrival in Houston. Special thanks are due to Kito Satomi, senior manager of international relations at the TNM, who skillfully coordinated the Tokyo National Museum's resources for the Arts of Japan Gallery project. Dr. Wada Hiroshi of the TNM Conservation Department has also been a great source of knowledge and assistance.

Many of the curators and experts also lent their extensive knowledge and expertise in writing the essays and entries for the catalogue to create this fine scholarly contribution to the understanding of Japanese art in the West. Aida Satoko of DNP Art Communications Co., Ltd., has played an instrumental role in supplying catalogue photography and copyright materials. Maiko Behr deserves recognition for diligently translating the essays and entries into English.

Many colleagues at the Museum of Fine Arts, Houston, helped to make the Arts of Japan Gallery and its related materials a reality. Thanks go to Gwendolyn H. Goffe, interim director, for her leadership, support, and long-term vision, and to Jack Eby, exhibition design director, for his thoughtful and remarkable sense of aesthetic. Bill Cochrane, exhibition designer, with Jack Eby planned and created the beautiful gallery space. Victoria Ramirez, the W. T. and Louise J. Moran Education Director, and Margaret Mims, associate education director, coordinated the robust educational programming in conjunction with the opening of the Arts of Japan Gallery. Jon Evans, head librarian, provided great support in acquiring the needed books and research material for the writing of the didactic material for the Arts of Japan Gallery. Felicia Yao, curatorial assistant of Asian art, organized the many details of the project and corresponded with the various people and institutional entities involved. Elspeth Patient, former administrative assistant to the Asian Art Department, handled the clerical and administrative matters related to the exhibition and catalogue, and new administrative assistant Esmeralda Salinas followed up on all tasks that needed to be completed with great attention to detail.

Julie Bakke, chief registrar, Geoffrey Dare, senior assistant registrar of incoming loans, and David Aylsworth, collections registrar, efficiently and thoroughly managed the transportation and storage of loan objects from Japan. Wynne Phelan, conservation director, Tina Tan, assistant conservator of works on paper, Toshiaki Koseki, Carol Crow Conservator of Photography, and their colleagues in the Conservation Department at the MFAH have also been instrumental in the safe transport, conservation, and storage of the objects.

I am also grateful to Shemon Bar-Tal, chief technology officer, and Saurin Ganatra, software developer, from the IT Department of the MFAH for their support of this project. Special thanks also go to Brian Hill, audio-visual technician, and his colleagues in the MFAH Audio-Visual Department.

Many thanks also to Dave Webb, security director, and his impressive team for their continued assistance. In the Image Library, Marty Stein oversaw the cataloging and organization of all the photography for the project. Under the supervision of Dale Benson, chief preparator, and Michael Kennaugh, senior preparator and administrator, the MFAH Preparations Department handled the movement of the art pieces with its usual excellence in care and professionalism. Diane Lovejoy, publications director, and Heather Brand, editor, lent their expert insight and sensibility to the content, layout, design, and production of this catalogue.

The development of the Arts of Japan Gallery was generously supported by various members of the Houston community, including Nanako and Dale Tingleaf, Penny and Paul Loyd, Donna Fujimoto Cole, Drs. Ellin and Robert Grossman, Akemi and Yasuhiko Saitoh, Miwa S. Sakashita and John R. Stroehlein, Taeko and Nobuya Tomita, and Nozomi and Ryuji Watanabe, as well as by major corporate sponsors, the Japan Business Association of Houston, Mitsui & Company (U.S.A.), Inc., Mitsubishi Corporation, Sumitomo Corporation of America, GE Energy, Gulf States Toyota, Inc., Mitsubishi International Corporation–Houston Branch, Satake USA Inc., and Toshiba International Corporation. A heartfelt thanks goes to Valerie Greiner, director of special gifts, for her hard work and diligence in leading the gallery's fundraising efforts.

The MFAH's Asian Art Subcommittee and the Friends of Asian Art support group have been at the core of the Asian Art Department at the Museum of Fine Arts, Houston. Without their generous support from the outset, this project, and many others over the years, would not have been possible.

The Arts of Japan Gallery, though, would have been impossible without the steadfast support of Dr. Peter C. Marzio, late director of the MFAH. His powerful vision gave the Asian Art Department the momentum that this substantial plan required. Though he was not able to witness the opening of the Arts of Japan Gallery, Dr. Marzio's legacy will continue to live on in these new permanent galleries for the museum's collections of Asian art.

The Arts of Japan Gallery is the latest in the MFAH's plan to reinstall its Asian galleries. The successful opening of the Arts of Korea Gallery in 2007 was followed with the opening of the Nidhika and Pershant Mehta Arts of India Gallery in 2009, and the Ting Tsung and Wei Fong Chao Arts of China Gallery in 2010. The triumphant opening of the Arts of Japan Gallery marks the final chapter of this reinstallation effort, which will profoundly change the way that Asian art is viewed and displayed.

Christine Starkman
Curator, Asian Art, Ancient to Contemporary
The Museum of Fine Arts, Houston

Preface

Christine Starkman

In March of 1900, five women organized the first meeting of the Houston Public School Art League, an organization to promote arts and culture in the city's schools. One of these women, Emma Richardson Cherry, who had attended the Académie Julian and had visited Claude Monet's colony at Giverny, was influenced by the Impressionists' enthusiasm for Japanese art. In 1906, she hosted an exhibit of "Japanese prints, embroideries, and curios" at the local Fannin School.[1] In addition to the exhibition, the Ladies Reading Club, which shared many civic-minded members with the league, gave papers and talks on Japanese subjects. The league's activities soon expanded to include much larger plans—plans for a permanent art museum for Houston. Land was secured, and the groundbreaking, in 1923, marked the beginning of what was to become the first building of the Museum of Fine Arts, Houston. The museum opened to the public the following year. Since that time, the museum has continued to grow, along with its collections and community partnerships.

According to the museum's records, the first example of Japanese art to enter the MFAH's collection was a piece of nineteenth-century Satsuma-ware porcelain, donated in 1935 by Mrs. Augusta Jones. However, several decades would pass before the museum was able to create a department devoted exclusively to the arts of Asia in 1980. That same year, the department secured a major acquisition: a pair of seventeenth-century Japanese screens with scenes from the *Tale of Genji*. Just two years later, Peter C. Marzio joined the MFAH as its new director, and he would ultimately have an important role in shaping the museum's collection and growth. His leadership led to the completion of the Lillie and Hugh Roy Cullen Sculpture Garden, designed by prominent Japanese American sculptor and designer Isamu Noguchi, which opened with fanfare in 1986.

The museum's holdings of Japanese art grew in the following years. In 1989, the Japan Business Association of Houston began an important partnership with the museum with the purchase of Japanese ceramics, paintings, and prints for the collection. The year 1990 marked the first meeting of the MFAH's Asian Art Subcommittee, which advises the museum in its acquisitions and includes museum Trustees and invited leaders from the Houston community. In 1992, the Brown Foundation Accessions Endowment Fund generously supported the purchase of a fifteenth-century sculpture of a seated Amida Buddha figure. The museum's endowment funds also made possible many other acquisitions of important Japanese paintings and sculptures. With these acquisitions came the need for exhibition space, and, in 1997, a three-thousand-square-foot gallery was opened as a dedicated space for the Asian art collection.

More recently, in 2003, Dr. Marzio, Asian Art Subcommittee members John B. Goodman and Mickey Rosenau, and I had the honor of launching the Friends of Asian Art, a support group devoted to the acquisition of major works of art from Asia for the museum. Since its founding, this group has acquired important works from India, Thailand, Cambodia, and China. Others supported the MFAH's endeavors as well. In 2006, Dr. Marjorie Horning created the Elizabeth S. and Marjorie G. Horning Asian Art Accessions Endowment Fund specifically for the purchase of Asian art.

In the past few years, Dr. Marzio determined that the museum's Asian art galleries needed to be reconceived and reinstalled, and I had the pleasure of working closely with him to bring about the necessary changes. Dr. Marzio clearly saw the need to make the ancient works of art more accessible by including modern and contemporary works in the same exhibition space, creating a new paradigm for how Asian art could be experienced. The first of the Asian galleries to be completed was the Arts of Korea Gallery, which opened in 2007. Thanks to generous support from the Korea Foundation, Korean corporations, and Houston's own Korean community, the museum was able to secure long-term loans of treasured works of art from the National Museum of Korea. Local community support was also crucial to the opening of the Nidhika and Pershant Mehta Arts of India Gallery in 2009 and the Ting Tsung and Wei Fong Chao Arts of China Gallery in 2010, which also marked the beginning of the museum's Portal Project. For this latest initiative, the MFAH plans to commission international contemporary artists to develop unique works of art to enhance the various Asian art galleries. The Portal Project is designed to create a visual narrative that connects the ideas of the past, present, and future. For the Ting Tsung and Wei Fong Chao Arts of China Gallery, contemporary artist Cai Guo-Qiang ignited gunpowder drawings on panels to produce a large-scale Chinese-style landscape and garden to cover the walls of that gallery. Other artists selected for commissions include Do Ho Suh for the Arts of Korea Gallery and Anish Kapoor for the Nidhika and Pershant Mehta Arts of India Gallery.

Now, more than a hundred years after the women of the Houston Public School Art League gathered to view and appreciate Japanese art, the Museum of Fine Arts, Houston, is celebrating the opening of a dedicated space to the arts of Japan. This long-anticipated Arts of Japan Gallery will mark the final stage in the effort to reinstall the museum's Asian art galleries. This latest gallery would not have been possible without the support of the museum's Trustees, Houston and Japanese community members, and the spectacular works of art on loan from the collection of the Tokyo National Museum. The leadership and vision of Peter C. Marzio (1982–2010) was crucial in bringing this project to fruition, and his legacy lives on in these galleries. By bringing art from around the world to Houston, and by honoring connections with Houston and international communities, the MFAH will continue to serve as a place for all people, as Dr. Marzio intended.

Note

1. From the historical records of the Houston Public School Art League, Houston Art League 1900–1924, p. 17, in the collection of the Museum of Fine Arts, Houston.

The History and Collection of the Tokyo National Museum

Matsumoto Nobuyuki

The Tokyo National Museum is located in the eastern part of Tokyo on the Ueno plateau. The larger area surrounding it is known as Ueno Onshi (Imperial Gift) Park and is covered with trees, most notably the rows of cherry trees lining its walks. Throughout this vast area are various institutions and cultural facilities, including museums, a zoo, theaters and music halls, universities and schools, research institutions, temples and shrines, and restaurants, creating a widely beloved community cultural zone.

The Tokyo National Museum stands on the former site of the abbot's residence of Kan'eiji, built in 1625, the family temple of the Tokugawa shogun who governed Japan in the Edo period (1603–1868). Covering a total area of roughly one hundred thousand square meters, the premises are graced by five exhibition buildings: the Honkan (Japanese Gallery), Tōyōkan (Asian Gallery), Hyōkeikan, Heiseikan, and the Gallery of Hōryūji Treasures.

As of March 2010, the collection of the Tokyo National Museum numbers roughly 113,000 entries of objects. The collection covers a wide range of artistic and historical objects, including paintings, calligraphies, sculpture, metalwork, arms and armor, ceramics, glass, wood and lacquerware, textiles, and architectural models. Not limited to art items, the collection also includes archaeological artifacts and historical and anthropological materials as well as large numbers of related books and manuscripts. Geographically, the collection's focus is on Japan, but it also spans the various regions of Asia and beyond, reaching as far as the Americas, Europe, Oceania, and even Africa. Just under ninety objects in the collection are designated National Treasures, and more than six hundred and twenty are Important Cultural Properties; thus, the museum houses approximately 10 percent of Japan's designated cultural properties. Groups of several pieces or even several dozen pieces are often counted collectively as a single entry, and at times—as, for example, in the case of archaeological artifacts uncovered together from a single tomb site—several thousand pieces are accessioned together as one entry. Taking this into consideration, the number of individual pieces in the Tokyo National Museum collection in fact reaches closer to one million objects, making it the largest museum collection in Japan both in terms of quality as well as quantity.

The history of the Tokyo National Museum is a direct measure of the evolution of the modern museum in Japan. It begins with the opening of an exposition of domestic items and curios held at the Taiseiden Hall of the Confucian temple Yushima Seidō in Tokyo in 1872, in the fifth year after the new Meiji government replaced the Edo shogunate in 1868. This event demonstrated to the Japanese people the richness of their land and its history and culture and also served as preparation for Japan's participation in the Vienna World's Fair, which was planned for the following year. Thus, one of its main goals was to support efforts toward the establishment of a modern nation-state and the Ministry of Education Museum (what would become today's Tokyo National Museum), which was formed as the institution that would play the leading role in holding these expositions.

In 1873, the year following the first exposition, seven facility buildings were established and moved to Uchiyamashitamachi (now Uchisaiwaichō in Tokyo's Chiyoda ward) both to house collections and to offer periodic exhibits to the public. This was the first museum in Japan. About the same time, the expansion of various activities led to the construction of a new gallery at the museum's current location on the site of the Kan'eiji abbot's residence in 1882. The new Western-style brick building was designed by the English architect Josiah Conder (1852–1920), a professor at the Imperial College of Engineering who had been invited to Japan to build Western architecture. In the 1880s, at about the time when this new building was opened, the Ministry of Education Museum was a comprehensive facility that housed a collection that included animals, plants, and minerals, and covered all fields of the natural sciences as well as art and decorative art objects. Along with its academic function, it also helped advance the modernization of Japan's industrial policies.

In 1889, when the Imperial Museum of Nara and the Imperial Museum of Kyoto were established, the name of the Ministry of Education Museum was changed to the Imperial Museum. The departments of history, art, and decorative arts formed the core of the Imperial Museum activities; they collected both Asian and Western art, and surveys of shrine and temple treasures further enriched the collection. In 1900, the museum's name was changed again to the Tokyo Imperial

Household Museum, and at that point the collection of art and decorative art objects along with historical materials—not including the natural-history collections—totaled 52,309 items. Ten years later, the number reached 75,359 items. Consequent to the growth of the collection, the Hyōkeikan was opened in 1909 as an exhibition hall for displaying objects of fine and decorative art. This hall not only housed regular exhibitions of fine and decorative art objects but also served as the venue for a number of special exhibitions and later provided space for the display of Japanese archaeological artifacts, which played an important role in the museum's activities until the opening of the Heiseikan in 1999.

Incidentally, 1923 was a year of major misfortunes for the Imperial Household Museum. The Great Kanto Earthquake, one of the biggest earthquakes in the history of Japan, demolished the original Honkan designed by Conder, and the cultural properties and specimens that had been on display also suffered substantial damage. In the course of recovery from the disaster, the zoo associated with the Imperial Household Museum was gifted to the city of Tokyo in 1924, and the museum gradually shifted its emphasis toward defining itself as an art museum by enacting such changes as transferring the natural-history department, with its core collection of animals, plants, and minerals, to the Tokyo Museum (today the National Museum of Nature and Science, Tokyo) the following year. Some time was needed, however, to rebuild the collapsed main building, and the new Honkan—the current building—was finally opened in 1938.

With the opening of the current Honkan, the museum positioned itself all the more clearly as an art museum dealing primarily with Japanese and Asian art. The Honkan and Hyōkeikan hosted a diverse array of exhibitions on an annual basis, including an exhibition of Imperial Treasures and other exhibitions of Japanese arts such as *ukiyo-e*, fashion, and *haniwa*, as well as those of Chinese ceramics and other subjects.

Later, the museum's activities were suspended due to the evacuation of the collections and the closing of the galleries resulting from the chaos of World War II. When the war ended and the new Constitution of Japan was enacted in 1947, the Imperial Household Museum came under the jurisdiction of the Ministry of Education and quickly achieved a fresh start as the National Museum. With the ratification of the Law for the Protection of Cultural Properties and the launch of the National Commission for the Protection of Cultural Properties in 1950, the National Museum became an auxiliary organ of that institution, and in 1952 acquired its present name, the Tokyo National Museum.

Upon this fresh renewal, the Tokyo National Museum started to co-organize a number of exhibitions with newspapers and other media companies, an endeavor that continues to this day. In addition to exhibitions of Japanese and Asian arts, the museum has also held more than ninety exhibitions of art from various foreign countries, such as the Henri Matisse exhibition of 1951 and the

Leonardo da Vinci exhibition of 2007. By introducing a wide range of foreign arts and cultures, the museum has made a great contribution to expanding the knowledge of the Japanese people in those fields. In addition to such co-organized exhibitions, the Tokyo National Museum has also organized its own planned exhibitions. Several of these exhibitions, such as the Mona Lisa exhibition of 1974, which drew 1,500,000 visitors, and the Tutankhamun exhibition of 1965, which drew 1,300,000 visitors, have seen incredible success, attesting to the vital role that the Tokyo National Museum has played culturally in Japan's postwar reconstruction and in its growth to become the economically mature country that it is today.

As mentioned, the scale and variety as well as the frequency of the museum's exhibitions have gradually expanded from the end of World War II to the present, and its exhibition facilities have expanded in keeping with these activities. In 1964, the Gallery of Hōryūji Treasures (the former facility designed by the Ministry of Construction Kantō Region Construction Bureau) opened exclusively for exhibiting the treasures donated by Hōryūji temple. Next, in 1968, the Tōyōkan (designed by Taniguchi Yoshirō) opened, making possible the permanent exhibition of cultural properties of various regions of Asia from ancient times to the present. In addition, a public Research and Information Center facility, housing historical documents, reference books, and photographic materials, was also opened in 1984. This center made it possible for scholars and educators as well as publishers, the press, and other professionals to obtain easy access to the various resources in the Tokyo National Museum collection, further solidifying its function as a cultural facility. More recently, in 1999, the new Gallery of Hōryūji Treasures and Heiseikan opened successively, bringing the total number of large-scale exhibition and research facilities on the Tokyo National Museum premises to six.

For the roughly one hundred forty years since its establishment, Japan's oldest and largest museum has conducted wide-ranging activities, from the standard collecting, exhibiting, conserving, and researching of cultural artifacts to conducting outreach and education programs, producing publications, providing access to research data and intercultural exchange, and various other activities expected of a museum. The Tokyo National Museum has always played a leading role in its field in Japan, keeping step with the many changes the country has undergone from early modern times until the present day. As a result, it has firmly established a position as an institution of Japanese culture and art, and in most recent years has welcomed an average of approximately two million visitors annually. The Tokyo National Museum appeals to a wide audience, not only domestically but also internationally, in an ongoing effort to promote understanding of its collection and history. With a vision toward the future, the museum continues to strive to become an ideal museum. In light of these efforts, it is our sincere hope that the opening of the Arts of Japan Gallery at the Museum of Fine Arts, Houston, will contribute to providing the American people the opportunity to join us in drawing one step closer toward a mutual understanding of our cultures.

Buddhist Art and Courtly Elegance

Shimatani Hiroyuki

THE RISE AND DEVELOPMENT OF BUDDHISM

In the middle of the sixth century, a bronze figure of Buddha and a number of sutra scrolls were brought to Japan from the Korean kingdom of Paekche.[1] This event marked the first official arrival of Buddhism in Japan. Soon after, the powerful Soga clan became devout adherents of Buddhism, leading to its later adoption at the imperial court. Before long, individuals possessing various specialized skills also arrived in Japan and contributed to the construction of Buddhist temples and of large numbers of ornaments for adorning Buddha statues. These events established the foundation for Buddhism to take root in Japan. In the Nara period, Buddhist ideology became the basis of governing the country, and the casting of the Great Buddha at Tōdaiji, which still survives today, and the construction of the Great Buddha Hall that houses it were undertaken as national projects. In addition, state monasteries (*kokubunji*) and nunneries (*kokubunniji*) were built in each of the more than sixty provinces of Japan with the aim of spreading the faith, and large numbers of Buddha sculptures were produced. Another national project involved the production of numerous copies of the *Issaikyō*, the complete canon of the Buddha's teachings.[2] In this way, Buddhism spread widely throughout Japan as a result of official government policies. The reception of Buddhism led at the same time to further absorption of the latest continental culture, leading Japanese culture to advance rapidly during this period.

However, the capital was moved to Heiankyō (modern-day Kyoto) in 794 in an effort to reform a government that had become too closely entangled with Buddhism and that had fallen into corrupt practices. The capital would remain there until it was relocated to Tokyo with the Meiji Restoration in 1868.

In the early Heian period, monks such as Kūkai (774–835) and Saichō (767–822) traveled to China and studied Esoteric Buddhism, which they introduced to Japan. The esoteric tradition was a new interpretation of Buddhism that emphasized the expression of Buddhist doctrine in tangible physical forms. Consequently, a new type of Esoteric Buddhist art was born. The Important Cultural Property *Seated Dainichi Nyorai* (Plate 5) is an example of one such artwork. It depicts Dainichi Nyorai, a deity akin to the sun who stands at the center of the universe, seated on a pedestal in the shape of a lotus flower. The lotus was believed to be sacred for its ability to produce a beautiful blossom in spite of growing out of the mud. Dainichi Nyorai's figure is majestically adorned with *kirikane* (finely cut strips of gold leaf), and his noble form and construction reflect the mid-Heian-period preference for the culture of *miyabi*, or courtly elegance.

The late Heian to Kamakura periods witnessed the spread of a belief in the coming era of *Mappō*, which was to begin in the year 1052, two thousand years after Buddha's death. It was thought that, during that degenerate era, neither the acts nor teachings of Buddha would be transmitted. At this time, there was also a blossoming of Pure Land faith, the belief in rebirth in a Western Paradise, where Amida Nyorai was believed to reside.[3] Rebirth in the Pure Land was believed to release one from all suffering to enjoy a life of eternal contentment in a beautiful, ideal utopia. The production of temple structures and artworks was pursued enthusiastically, inspired by such beliefs. The Phoenix Hall of Byōdōin, a temple located near Kyoto, is a well-known example of an Amida hall based on this philosophy.

Also during this time, the teachings of the *Lotus Sutra* (*Hokekyō*) drew widespread devotion. Reading the scripture was believed to constitute a pious act, and the sutra also advocated the possibility of attaining enlightenment by copying out its textual passages by hand (in the "Hosshibon" chapter) and further proclaimed the potential of salvation for women (in the "Daibabon" chapter). Those seeking the protection of Buddha through these teachings turned to fervent recitation and copying of the *Lotus Sutra*, and, in time, specific rituals were established for dedicating these sutra copies to temples.[4] Lavishly decorated sutras were produced based on the teaching that the earth of the Pure Land paradise was lapis lazuli and adorned with "seven gems" (gold, silver, pearls, agate, rock crystal, coral, and lapis lazuli).[5] These sutras were embellished on their covers and endpapers, directly on the sutra papers, and even on their rollers, cords, or title cartouches. An example is *Daitō Saiiki ki*, one of the Chūsonji scrolls (Plate 2), with its alternating columns of softly brushed gold and silver characters on indigo-dyed paper, complete with sensitive and refined paintings on the cover and endpapers. This work is an example of the type of elaborate decorative sutras produced through the convergence of the intense faith and heightened aesthetic sensibilities of the people of the time.

A wide variety of Buddhist implements were also produced for decorating the halls where Buddha figures were enshrined. The *Kasha (Incense Burner)* and *Set of Six Ritual Bowls* (Plate 7), *Five-pronged Vajra Bell* (Plate 8), *Five-pronged Vajra Club* (Plate 9), *Bell with Handle in the Shape of a Stupa* (Plate 10), and *Incense Burner with Handle* (Plate 11) are objects used in Esoteric Buddhist rituals. Among them, the kasha and incense burner with handle were used when making offerings of incense, the most important part of ritual offerings to Buddha. Other kinds of offerings included dedicating flowers or lighting candles. Ringing the vajra bell during esoteric rituals was believed to summon and delight the various deities to whom offerings were being made. The vajra club was originally an ancient Indian weapon that was adopted by Esoteric Buddhism as an object that destroyed worldly desires and became a symbol of the essential teachings of Buddha. Additional ritual implements include objects such as a bronze tray on which the club and bell are placed.

Over time, various sects of what was called new Kamakura Buddhism were formed, while the older Buddhist sects poured their energy into the revival of their own sects and temple buildings. Amid such trends, the subjects depicted in Buddhist art grew more diverse and evolved, exhibiting the influence of Song-dynasty styles or attempts to revive Nara-period styles. Typical works of the period include sculptures and portraits of the founders of various Buddhist sects, illustrated scrolls depicting the life stories of high priests, or handscrolls illustrating the miraculous events or origin stories of specific temples and shrines. The *Nirvana Painting* (Plate 4) depicts the scene of the deathbed of Buddha. Bodhisattvas and disciples as well as numerous animals gather together to lament the sad event. Such paintings would have been used on the occasion of the *Nehan-e* (Nirvana ceremony) memorial service, held on the fifteenth day of the second month of the Japanese lunar calendar, the anniversary of Buddha's death.[6]

Even in the times that followed, Buddhism continued to play a major role in Japanese culture. Although the Japanese are polytheistic, Buddhist altars are placed in many homes and, whether one is conscious of it or not, honoring one's ancestors through memorial rites becomes unavoidable as one approaches a certain prescribed age. Even today, various Buddhist customs, such as visiting ancestral graves at the time of the spring and autumn equinoxes and sending off the ancestral spirits or participating in *bon-odori* dances during the summer *obon* season remain deeply rooted in Japanese life.

COURTLY BEAUTY

A variety of cultural and technical innovations, beginning with Buddhism, as previously mentioned, were brought to Japan through cultural exchange with China and Korea. Following the successive emperors of the Nara period, Emperor Saga (788–842) of the early Heian period was particularly enamored of Chinese Tang culture. Consequently, his court adopted a great variety of ceremonies and functions emulating Tang models. In addition to the increasing popularity of Chinese literature and history studies, Tang culture further impacted all aspects of life, from customs of receiving guests at court to the holding of Chinese poetry gatherings, as well as men's and women's clothing styles and leisure activities, among other aspects. This admiration for the advanced culture of China led to devoted imitation of Tang culture in Japan from the Nara period to the beginning of the Heian period.

THE CONCEPT OF MIYABI AND CULTIVATION OF THE ARISTOCRACY

By the middle of the Heian period, however, a variety of issues arose that could not be addressed by a legal system modeled after the Tang Chinese form of government, and a series of amendments and new government offices were established in response to changing times. These measures were taken to adapt the Chinese system to the reality of Japanese society.

Meanwhile, Tang China, which had enjoyed great prosperity and had been the object of Japan's admiration, fell into a period of upheaval as the result of, among other things, the An-Shi Rebellion (755–763) at the hands of An Lushan and Shi Siming. Following a diplomatic dispatch in 838, several scheduled envoys from Japan were cancelled in succession. Then finally, in 894, Sugawara Michizane (845–903), the appointed ambassador to Tang China, proposed that such missions be abolished completely. Thus, this era saw a shift from indiscriminate devotion to

Chinese culture to a decrease in exposure to new stimuli, both institutional as well as material, from the continent. Eventually, Japanese culture—like its political system—also transformed to become more compatible with its own topography and national character. During this period of court culture, centered on the imperial household and its regents and advisors, the concept of the aesthetic of miyabi was born, and literature, arts, and decorative arts based on this aesthetic gradually blossomed into a unique "Japanese-style" (*wayō*) culture.[7]

Where did the interests of the cultivated elite of the Heian period lie? And what kind of education provided the foundation for their culture?[8] A document explaining the details of various aspects of daily life at court, written by an exemplary nobleman of the early Heian period, Fujiwara Morosuke (908–960), for his male descendants, offers a glimpse at the times.[9] Not only does this document allow us to understand Morosuke's personal philosophy and his character, but it also serves as a valuable reference for understanding the lifestyle and education system of aristocrats of the day more broadly. According to his treatise, reading historical texts and biographies was of primary importance to becoming a properly educated adult. Next in importance was learning calligraphy, and only after that, he wrote, was leisure finally allowed. These writings clearly show his strong parental desire for a sound upbringing for his children. Later, Fujiwara Yorinaga (1120–1156), a late-Heian-period courtier during the reign of Emperor Toba, proposed Minamoto Arihito (1103–1147) as an example of the ideal man—one of exceptional good looks, skilled in music, and talented in calligraphy and *waka* poetry.[10] From these various sources, it would appear that the ideal male aristocrat of the Heian period conducted government affairs and ceremonies and at the same time had a thorough knowledge of the Chinese classics and was skilled in cultural and fine arts such as Chinese and Japanese poetry, calligraphy, and music. In short, being proficient in all of these fields was crucial to achieving a high rank as a prominent courtier.

Many of these skills were indispensable to women's education as well. In Section 23 of her *Makura no sōshi* (Pillow Book), Sei Shōnagon lists the things that a princess should learn: first, calligraphy; second, the zither (*koto*) and other music, and third, recitation of all of the waka poems in *Kokinwakashū* (Collection of Poems, Ancient and Modern). "Kuniyuzuri, Part I" (The Succession) in volume 3 of *Utsubo monogatari* (The Tale of the Hollow Tree), describes ladies absorbed in writing practice until late into the night, and in Part I of *Hamamatsu Chūnagon monogatari* (The Tale of the Hamamatsu Middle Counselor), calligraphy is shown to be such a major part of daily life that writing practice is spoken of as being like a friend. From these examples, it is clear that writing practice, of all the various refinements, was considered to be of the greatest importance. Moreover, in *Genji monogatari* (The Tale of Genji) as well, calligraphic style and relative skill or lack thereof is mentioned numerous times. *Torikaebaya monogatari* (The Tale of the Changelings) further attests to the importance of painting and music practice, particularly the koto, in addition to calligraphy.

These various documents offer an understanding of just how important a part of the daily routine calligraphy practice was for men and women alike at the Heian court. The distinction between skillful and poor calligraphy was a matter of great concern for both men and women, as it continues to be to this day.

COURT NOBLES AND MUSIC

Ceremonies and annual events were of great importance to the court nobles, as previously mentioned. Gifts were often sent on those occasions, and the most highly prized gifts were model books of texts such as the *Kokinwakashū*, followed by famous musical instruments with a recognized provenance, such as lutes (*biwa*), zithers, and flutes (*fue*), and swift horses. Such gifts were not meant to be simply stored and treasured; they served a practical function as well. The decorated model books were admired and enjoyed, but they also served as examples to be emulated in calligraphy practice. Similarly, prize horses were admired for their beauty but were also carefully bred and paraded behind their owners by guards during ceremonies and annual events.[11] Musical instruments, likewise, were appreciated for their craftsmanship, but of course were also used for performing music, and pedigreed instruments were particularly highly esteemed as gifts because of the function they filled at specific ceremonies and musical gatherings. The *Shō (mouth-organ) called "Mura-chidori"* (Plate 12), *Ryūteki (dragon flute) called "Ashitazu"* (Plate 13), and *Hichiriki (flageolet-like instrument) called "Higurashi"* (Plate 14), featured in this catalogue, were treasured and passed down from the Kamakura period to the Edo period. They were indispensable to musical performances at court and have been cherished by later generations. Musical scores that document the ancient traditions are also necessary in order to perform music, and in Japan many precious musical scores have been passed down from the Heian period, including *Kagura wagon no hifu* (National Treasure, Yōmei Bunko Collection) and *Kinkafu* (dated 981, Important Cultural Property, Yōmei Bunko Collection). Even today, the Imperial Household Agency has a Music Department, which holds regular performances and preserves traditional *gagaku* music for today's generation.

THE DEVELOPMENT OF "JAPANESE STYLE"

Even after the Heian political administration was replaced by the samurai class in the Kamakura period, awareness of the miyabi concept remained central to Japanese culture. However, this concept became more refined over the ages and was elaborated in different art forms with the passing of time. From the Muromachi period to the Warring States period, Kyoto culture was disseminated to the provinces and spread in many layers of reception. Meanwhile, calligraphy remained fixed within a codified form that stressed the importance of tradition, resulting in a standardized writing style. In the following Azuchi-Momoyama period, encounters with various European cultures resulted in one of the most vibrant periods of creative diversity in Japan's history. In addition to examples of conventional calligraphy and Yamato-e (Japanese-style) paintings that emerged in the Heian period, numerous paintings and calligraphic works in eccentric styles also survive from this time. For example, Emperor Goyōzei (1571–1617) has left examples of calligraphic works imbued with tradition but exhibiting a fascinating charm that is deeply influenced by the ethos of this era. This development brought new life to a world of calligraphy and painting that had been rigidly bound by tradition. His *Characters "Dragon" and "Tiger"* (Plate 3) may appear unconventional, but at the same time, the upward churning brushwork retains characteristics of the traditional Daishi School, based on the calligraphic style of the monk Kūkai (also known as Kōbō Daishi). This work is an example of strong individualism grounded in tradition.

CONCLUSION

As already mentioned, the Japanese people's deep faith in the gods and Buddhism is undeniably evident in their arts. It has further been demonstrated that the emperor-centered court aristocracy not only admired the ability to conduct government affairs and official ceremonies, but also valued skill in all areas of arts and culture, including knowledge of the Chinese classics, Chinese and Japanese poetry, calligraphy, and music. Furthermore, the annual functions and culture that formed the basis of daily life at court were not just for the nobility; they constituted the very essence of Japanese culture. The selection of works presented in this catalogue and related exhibition brings into focus these two key elements in Japanese art—Buddhist faith and courtly elegance.

Notes

1. According to the *Jōgū Shōtoku Hōō teisetsu* (Biography of Prince Shōtoku) and *Gangōji engi* (Legends of Gangōji Temple), this occurred in the year 538; in the *Nihon shoki*, it is recorded as the tenth month of 552.
2. Issaikyō is a compilation of scriptures—also known as the *Daizōkyō*, or *Tripitaka*—that includes three classes: *sutras*, which record the teachings of the Buddha, *vinayas*, which outline the rules and precepts to be observed, and *abhidharmas*, which serve as commentaries on the Buddha's teachings. The *Tang-dynasty Kaiyuan shijiao lu* (Catalogue of Buddhist Scripture Compiled in the Kaiyuan Era) lists the total number of volumes as 5,048.
3. In *Ōjoyōshū*, his essays on rebirth into paradise, Genshin (also Eshin Sōzu, 942–1017) advocated that if one invoked the aid of Amida, the Buddha of Infinite Light, in this life, one could be reborn in the Pure Land paradise in the next.
4. In Japan, the *Lotus Sutra* served as the main scripture of the Tendai sect, which was founded by Saichō and based at Enryakuji temple. Through the Tendai sect, *Lotus Sutra* belief spread widely among the nobility.
5. See Shimatani Hiroyuki, "Sōshokukyō no rekishi" ["The History of Decorated Sutras"], in *Saichō to Tendai no kokuhō* [Faith and Syncretism: Saichō and Treasures of Tendai], exhibition catalogue (Tokyo: Tokyo National Museum and Yomiuri Shimbunsha, 2005).
6. Translator's note: Premodern dates are cited here according to the Japanese lunar calendar, which ran approximately three to seven weeks behind the Western calendar. The fifteenth day of the second month would correspond approximately to March or early April.
7. See Shimatani Hiroyuki, "Wayō no sho" ["Japanese-style calligraphy"], *Nihon no Bijutsu* [Japanese Art] 519 (August 2009).
8. For a further discussion, see Shimatani Hiroyuki, "Kyūtei kizoku no seikatsu to bunka" ["Lifestyle and Culture of the Court Nobility"], in *Kyūteinomiyabi* [Courtly Millennium—Art Treasures from the Konoe Family Collection] (Tokyo: Tokyo National Museum and NHK Promotions, 2008), 14–22.
9. *Kujō-dono yuikai* [Testament of Lord Kujō], vol. 1, from vol. 9 of the *Gunsho ruijū*, an Edo-period woodblock-printed bibliography of historical and literary texts.
10. In his diary, *Taiki*, entry of the third day of the second month, 1147.
11. From the Heian period onward, members of the imperial guards accompanied court nobles for their protection when they appeared in public. However, these men were not mere escorts, but were also often dancers and poets and thus were expected to be handsome and highly cultured as well.

The Japanese People and Waka Poetry

The Japanese People and Waka Poetry

Shimatani Hiroyuki

From the time it broke away from the larger genre of songs (*kayō*) in ancient times, *waka* poetry developed on its own as a distinct literary genre. In the Nara period (710–794), this type of poetry was composed widely, leading to the eventual compilation of the poetry anthology *Man'yōshū*, which included four thousand poems.

In the early Heian period, Emperor Saga (786–842) was more partial to Chinese culture, however, and implemented various ceremonies and functions emulating Tang Chinese models during his reign. In time, Tang culture permeated all aspects of life, from a blossoming of Chinese literature and history studies to new reception practices at the imperial palace, the holding of Chinese poetry gatherings, and even to Chinese clothing styles and leisure pastimes for both men and women. Waka poetry languished as a result of the popularity of Chinese literature in the Kōnin and Jōgan eras, and the public presentation of waka even fell into disfavor.[1]

By the mid-Heian period, Japan experienced a period of "Japanification" of government and culture, as it became less enchanted with Chinese culture and had decreased diplomatic relations with China. As a consequence, Japanese culture began to exhibit less and less influence from the continent. The first imperially commissioned waka poetry anthology, the *Kokinwakashū* (Collection of Poems, Ancient and Modern), exemplifies this trend.[2] With the decline in interest in Chinese culture, waka poetry now took center stage and stood on par with Chinese poetry.

In accordance with this trend of the nobility's adoration of things Japanese, waka poetry contests and gatherings were held frequently at court, and the ability to compose waka poetry skillfully became an important refinement for both men and women. Aristocratic lords and ladies would spend their days and nights in earnest study of waka alongside other cultural pursuits in their efforts to succeed at court. As a result, various types of poetic anthologies became very popular, including imperial collections, such as the *Gosenwakashū*, as well as privately compiled collections and compendia of poems by a single poet. Soon waka became an indispensable and central feature of classical court culture.

Waka poetry addressed a wide variety of subjects, such as the beauty of the changing of the seasons, the pain of separation, and the elation that comes with devotion to the gods and Buddha. Of course, the burning desires felt by men for women, and women for men, were also a particularly important topic.

While waka served as a field of study for cultivation and refinement by the court nobles and ladies-in-waiting, it was also an extremely important tool for drawing the attentions of the opposite sex. Upper-class men and women had hardly any opportunities to meet face-to-face, and had virtually no way to evaluate a person's merit or attractiveness—aside from rumor or hearsay—except through writing and waka poetry exchanges facilitated by an intermediary. For this reason, many imperial waka anthologies and personal poetry collections include large numbers of poems expressing the passionate feelings between men and women.

Such love poems were communicated through handwritten letters. The relative proficiency of one's handwriting was a topic of deep interest among the court nobles of the time. Exceptional calligraphers were highly regarded for this skill. While the content of the waka was of obvious importance, the beauty of the calligraphy also weighed heavily in the potential success of a romantic liaison. Someone receiving a waka poem would scrutinize both the content as well as the handwriting, and would raise a brush in reply only if it were deemed worthy on both counts.

Heian-period handscrolls and booklets written by skilled calligraphers are commonly referred to as *tehon* (copybooks). For example, the passage describing the preparations of trousseau accoutrements for Princess Akashi's introduction at court in the "Umegae" (A Branch of Plum) chapter of *Genji monogatari* (The Tale of Genji) mentions that the finest calligraphy scrolls were used as models for writing practice as well as for visual enjoyment as extravagant furnishings for decorating the mansion interiors. Such model books as personal accoutrements were the most treasured gifts one could receive at ceremonies and events, valued more than pedigreed musical instruments such as lutes, zithers, and flutes, and even more than horses. Therefore, when making copybooks, minute attention was given to the selection of writing papers, the finishing details of the wrapping cords or rollers of books and handscrolls, and even to the boxes in which they were stored, yet the calligraphy was the most carefully executed of all. Today, surviving copybooks of this type are collectively known as *kohitsu* (old writings). Originally, kohitsu was a word used to refer to the calligraphy of people of ancient times. The contents of these old writings were wide-ranging, and they reflected the tastes of the people of their time in all aspects, including in their decoration. They are also precious artifacts attesting to the love the nobles of the day felt for the art of poetry.

The *Man'yōshū* anthology was very highly esteemed, as was the first imperial waka poetry anthology, the *Kokinwakashū*. The Takamatsunomiya version of the *Man'yōshū* (Plate 1, annotated in the Genryaku era) in the Tokyo National Museum collection is an example of a model book that has been treasured as a courtly furnishing. This work is a supreme example of the expression of the miyabi aesthetic that was so beloved by the Heian aristocrats. It represents an indisputably magnificent collaboration between the literary art of waka and the visual art of calligraphy, with the added refinement of the pure and delicate art of decorative writing-paper design.

Waka addressed every aspect of Japanese life and, as a result, provided inspiration for designs in various art forms, including painting, costume design, lacquerware, and others. Key elements from famous waka poems were given visual expression in a variety of different ways. The most famous waka poems are so familiar that many Japanese have memorized them and thus are able to recognize subtle visual references to them in painted scenes, allowing for even greater depth of appreciation of other arts.

Waka poems express sentiments of the heart in a fixed form of five phrases of five, seven, five, seven, and seven syllables each, but even while adhering to this limited structure, they continue to seek to express diverse emotions in new ways. A poetic treatise by Fujiwara no Teika (1162–1241) states, "Newness in feeling is most important. In expressing this, one must choose words from tradition."[3] This notion was passed on from the great Muromachi-period scholar Sanjōnishi Sanetaka (1455–1537) to the tea master Takeno Jōō, and further to Sen no Rikyū, thus exerting a profound influence on the formation of the aesthetic that came to define the art of the tea ceremony. The highest tea masters held Fujiwara no Teika in great esteem, which contributed significantly, of course, to the role that poetry came to play in the aesthetics of the tea ceremony, and to the preservation of his attitude toward waka in future generations. Even today in Japan, it is considered proper to study the classics and master them before attempting to express one's own individuality and feelings. In other words, one's personal style of expression and creativity is built on a foundation of convention. This ideal defines the essence of Japanese culture, and it is surely one of the main reasons that waka is beloved and esteemed by so many Japanese people.

Notes

1. From the "Kana Preface" of the *Kokinwakashū*. Translator's note: English translation by Helen Craig McCullough, *Kokin Wakashū: The First Imperial Anthology of Japanese Poetry* (Stanford, CA: Stanford University Press, 1996), 5.

2. Commissioned by Emperor Daigo in 905 and compiled by Ki no Tsurayuki and others, it was completed about 914.

3. From the introduction to his *Eiga no taigai* (Essentials of Poetic Composition), c. 1222.

PLATE 1

1.

Man'yōshū, Vol. 9 (Takamatsunomiya version)

National Treasure
Heian period, 11th century
One of a set of twenty bound booklets, ink on paper

9 ¾ x 6 ¾ inches (25 x 17 cm)
Tokyo National Museum

This volume is one of a set of twenty bound booklets copied from a handscroll edition of the twenty-volume poetry anthology *Man'yōshū*. This booklet utilizes an eggshell-colored paper known as *torinoko*, characteristic of the Heian period, which is flecked with indigo- and violet-dyed fibers that form a cloudlike pattern and is ruled with pale ink lines. Originally, it was assembled in the "butterfly binding" technique, in which single-sided sheets were folded in half with the text on the inside and pasted back-to-back at the fold. However, because the booklet had been split into smaller volumes and some individual pages had become detached during its transmission, it was rebound with thread on top of the original binding.

The poems are written in the original *man'yōgana* characters, based on Chinese ideographs, in which the ancient *Man'yōshū* collection was conceived, inscribed alongside a transcription in the Japanese syllabic alphabet, hiragana. With the exception of one later addition in Volume 6, it was originally a complete set comprising calligraphy by more than ten different calligraphers. Given that the same calligrapher who inscribed the opening pages of Volume 1 in this collection also inscribed the *Wakan shō* (National Treasure, Yōmei Bunko Collection), the Group 3 *Kokinwakashū* segments known as Kōya-gire,[1] and other similar works, this *Man'yōshū* manuscript appears to date back to the end of the eleventh century. Known as the Genryaku collation, it takes its name from a colophon in Volume 20, which states that this version was examined and compared against another version in the year Genryaku 1 (1184).

Today, the Genryaku collation survives as an incomplete set in twenty fragmentary booklets in the Tokyo National Museum collection. There are additional segments that were detached from the booklets and divided among various families, such as the Arisugawa-gire and Naniwa-gire segments. This division and dispersal occurred in response to widespread demand from individuals who wanted to own an exceptional piece of calligraphy or to show calligraphic works in scroll form to guests at tea gatherings.

This work is considered one of the "Five Great Editions of the *Man'yōshū*" of the Heian period, along with the Katsura version, Ranshi (violet paper) version, Kanazawa version, and Tenji version. It is of particular importance because it has preserved the greatest number of poems and represents a collaboration of a number of accomplished calligraphers. **S.H.**

Note

1. The segments of the oldest surviving copy of the *Kokinwakashū* poetry collection, known as the Kōya-gire segments, are believed to have been the collaborative work of three different calligraphers. The sections attributed to each are known as Group 1, Group 2, and Group 3.

はなそみのよそ

をくしもとらんともおも

藤井連遷任上京時娘子贈

日者吾波孤悲牟奈名欲

咲山之峯上乃櫻花將
ろはれやまのをのへのさくらち
はこさみをおもそへ
笑來何時將散錫還有若

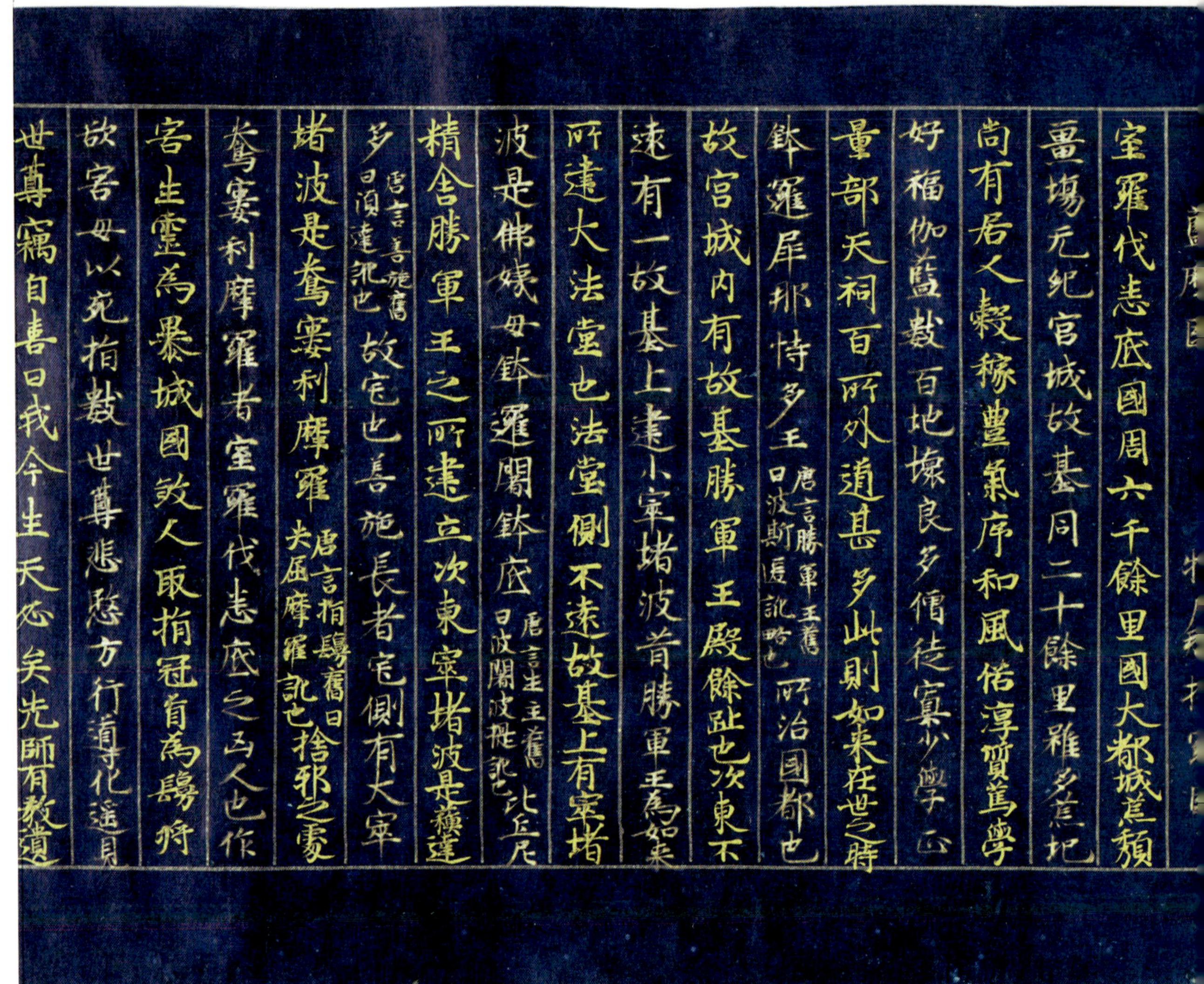

2.

Daitō Saiiki ki

(Record of the Chinese Priest Xuanzang's Journey to the West), Vol. 1

Important Cultural Property

Heian period, 12th century

One of a set of twelve handscrolls, gold and silver on indigo paper

With mounting:

10 ⅛–10 ⅜ inches (25.6–26.3 cm) x 251 ¾–569 ⅝ inches (639.3–1446.9 cm);

Without mounting:

10 x 424 ⅜ inches (25.3 x 1078.1 cm)

Tokyo National Museum

The *Daitō Saiiki ki* is an account of the travels of the Tang priest Xuanzang from the time he left Chang'an in 629 to tour China's western regions and India until his return in 645. It comprises a total of twelve volumes, and the Tokyo National Museum version survives in almost complete form with

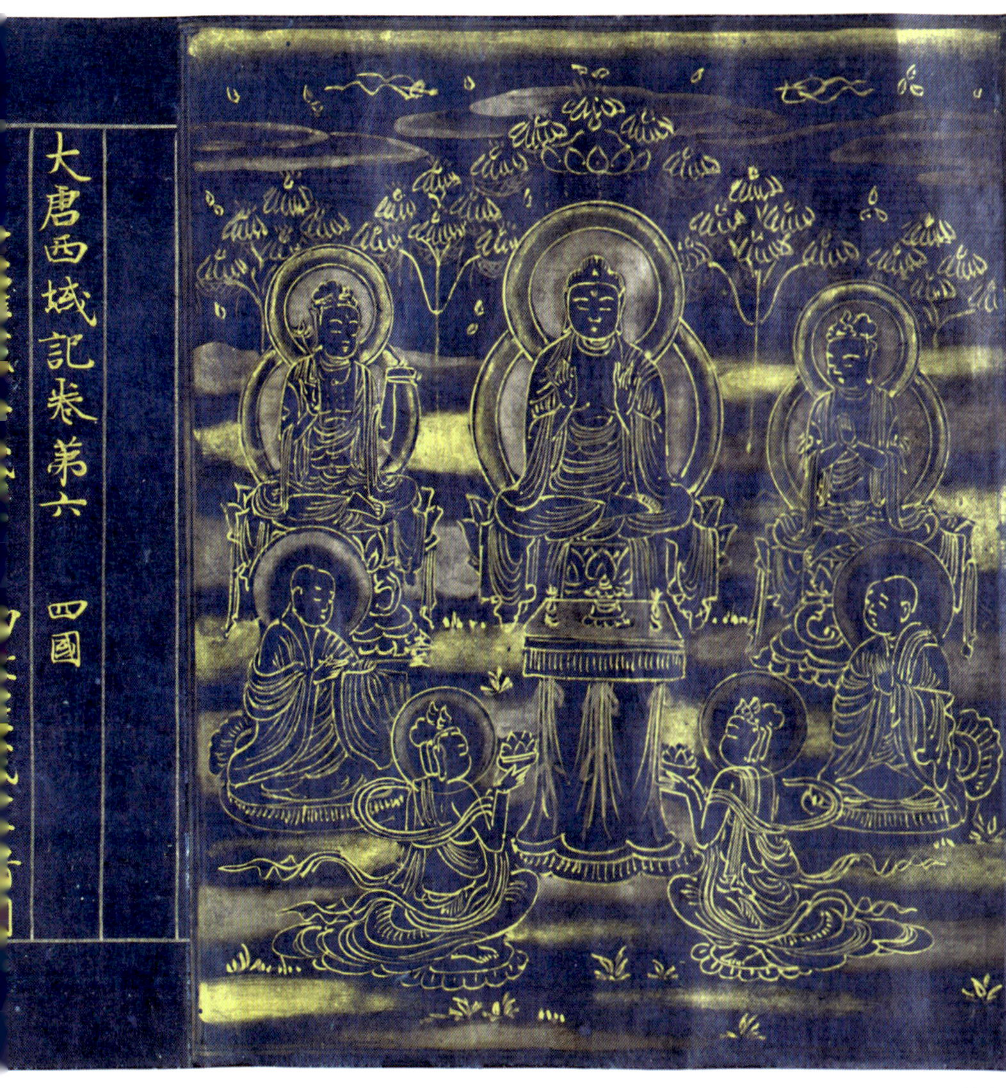

PLATE 2

only some minor losses. The text is inscribed in the form of a sutra copy in alternating lines of gold and silver pigment on indigo paper.

Between the years 1117 and 1119, Fujiwara Kiyohira (1056–1128), a powerful lord of the northeastern region of Japan, commissioned a copy of the complete Buddhist canon, or *Issaikyō*, totaling more than five thousand volumes. He did this to invoke divine support for the successful establishment of Chūsonji temple in Hiraizumi, in present-day Iwate Prefecture. He dedicated these scrolls to the temple on its completion ceremony in 1126, and they are now known collectively as the Chūsonji sutras. The majority of these sutras—a total of 4,296 volumes—were later transferred to Kongōbuji temple on Mt. Kōya, where they remain today.

Most of the sutra copies are written on plain paper with dark ink, but several, including this scroll, are known as decorated sutras, inscribed on papers dyed with indigo or purple, and traced in gold or silver ink. Intended to adorn the sutra text, such decorations were founded on the belief that the Western Paradise was covered in lapis lazuli and bedecked with gold and silver and other treasures. The covers are painted with *hōsōge* (mythical Buddhist flower) arabesques, and the endpapers of each scroll are painted in gold and silver with images of Buddha lecturing or with illustrations based on the text of the sutra, which serve as valuable records of the painting tradition of their time. **S.H.**

3.

Characters "Dragon" and "Tiger"

by Emperor Goyōzei (1571–1617)
Important Art Object
Azuchi-Momoyama period, 16th–17th century
Hanging scroll, ink on decorative paper

47 ⅝ x 21 inches (120.8 x 53.3 cm)
Tokyo National Museum

Emperor Goyōzei (1571–1617) was the 107th emperor of Japan and reigned between the Azuchi-Momoyama period and the early Edo period. Faced with the decline in authority of the imperial court, he worked to restore its dignity through the support of such powerful leaders as Toyotomi Hideyoshi (1536–1598) and Tokugawa Ieyasu (1542–1616). Celebrated for his love of scholarship, he studied Chinese classics under Funabashi Hidekata (1575–1614), and Japanese literature and philosophy with Hosokawa Yūsai (1534–1610). He even lectured on the Heian-period *Genji monogatari* (The Tale of Genji), the Kamakura-period poetic treatise *Eiga no taigai* (Essentials of Poetic Composition) by Fujiwara no Teika (1162–1241), and other literary subjects. His knowledge of the classics, both domestic and foreign, was deep, and he contributed greatly to the progress of scholarship during his time through projects such as the imperial publications of the Keichō era. He is also known for the prominent role that he played in court politics and culture. During Goyōzei's reign, the warlord Toyotomi Hideyoshi unified the country, and Japan enthusiastically pursued cultural exchange with foreign lands, while domestic economic activity thrived. The encounter with previously unknown European cultures resulted in an uncommon level of expansion in the area of creative production.

The sumptuous mood of this period extended even to works of calligraphy, and Emperor Goyōzei's writings in particular were considered by many to breathe new life into an art form that had been rigidly clinging to tradition. The two characters seen here, "dragon" and "tiger," appear at first glance to be quite unique, but the swirling stroke of the brush at the ends of the characters shows the influence of the traditional Daishi School style, based on the calligraphy of the renowned medieval priest Kōbō Daishi (Kūkai). The words "dragon" and "tiger" together embody a heroic ideal and were a favorite subject for emperors. Brilliant decorative paper with images of bridges, willow trees, and flowing water traced in gold and silver inks epitomizes the double allure of courtly elegance and profound individualism in Momoyama culture. **S.H.**

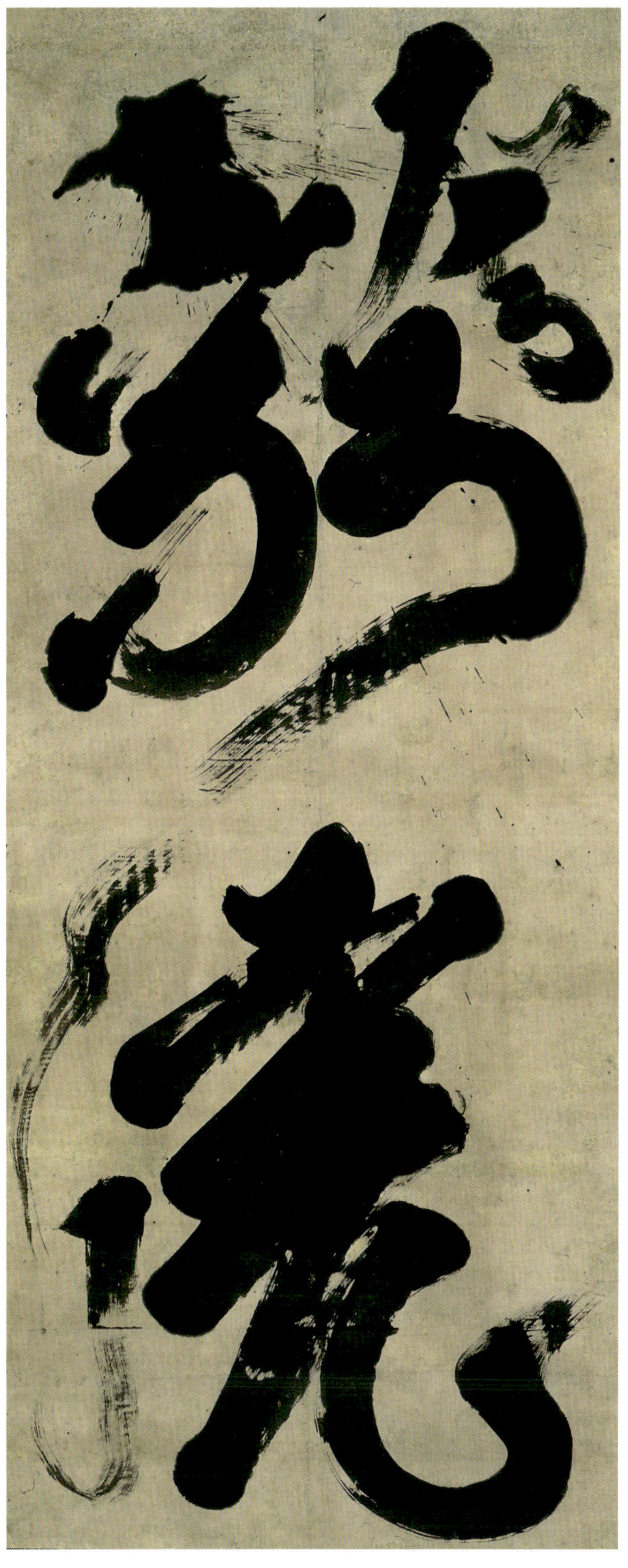

PLATE 3

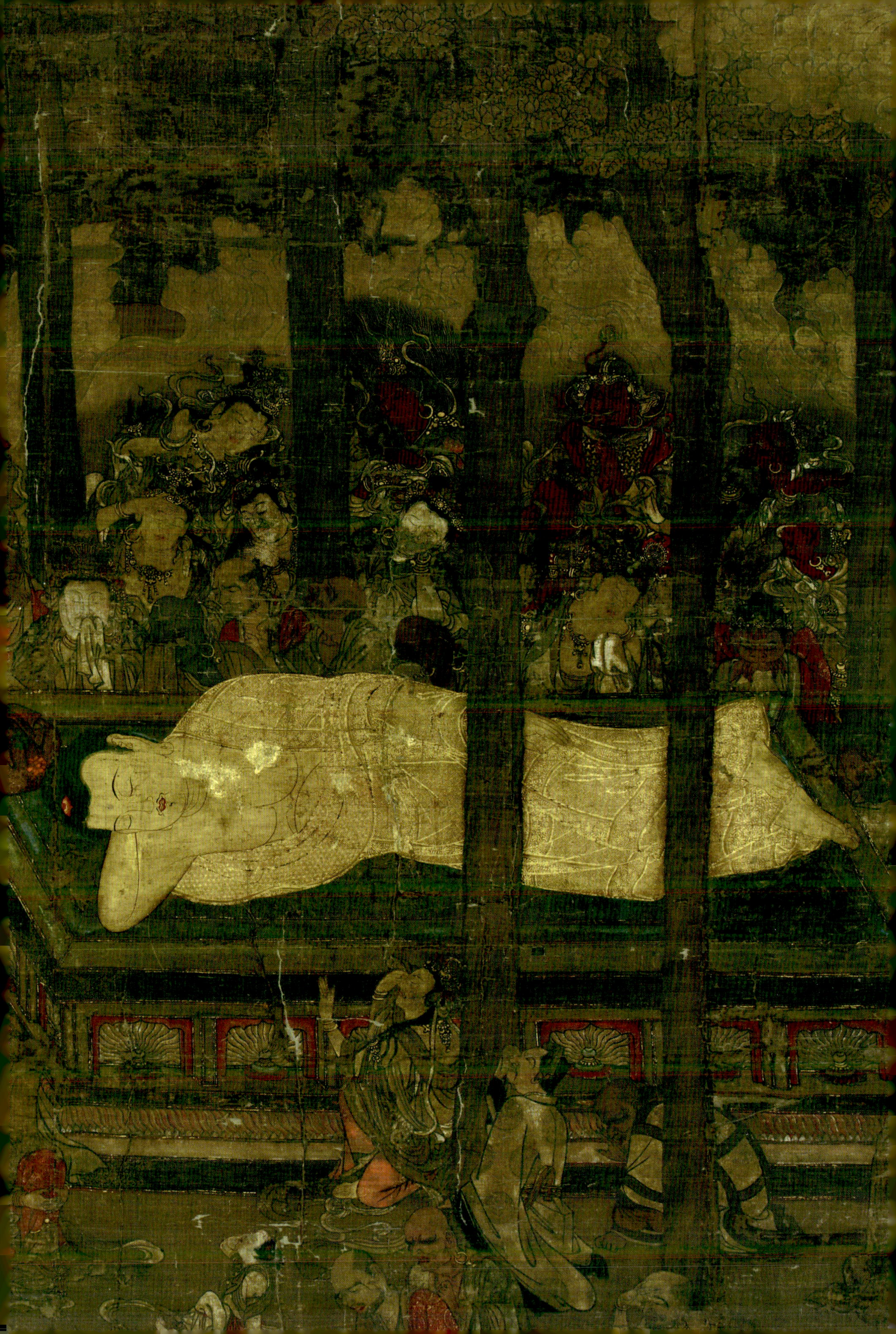

Nirvana Paintings in Japan

Nirvana Paintings in Japan

Seya Ai

Nirvana paintings are Buddhist images depicting the scene of the deathbed of Buddha Śākyamuni, the founder of Buddhism. The Sanskrit word *nirvana* literally means "blown out" and signifies the extinguishing of the flame of life, and, by extension, the death of a sage who has emancipated himself from desires and has attained enlightenment. The death of Buddha was different from death in its normal sense in that it signified release from various physical hardships and the attainment of eternal comfort. Nirvana paintings, while depicting the tragedy of Buddha's death, also conversely illustrate the moment of great liberation from earthly desires and woes, and constitute one of the most representative themes of Buddhist painting.

Now, let us imagine the last moment of Buddha's life. After entering the priesthood at age twenty-nine and practicing various austerities, Śākyamuni attained enlightenment while sitting in meditation under a bodhi tree. Following this experience, he embarked on a journey around various lands, where he offered spiritual guidance and led people to Buddhism for more than forty years. Ultimately, however, he fell seriously ill and passed away in a forest of sal trees in Kushinagar. Some Buddhist sutras explain that his death was caused by violent stomachaches from eating mushrooms offered to him by a blacksmith's son named Cunda. Foreseeing his own death, Śākyamuni lay down in a clearing with a pair of sal trees standing above him at each of the cardinal directions. According to legend, at the moment of his death, the sal trees surrounding him suddenly turned white, thus some Nirvana paintings illustrate this detail by depicting the trees in green and white. These sal trees are also considered a symbol of the impermanence of this world, as demonstrated in one of the opening lines of Japan's renowned Kamakura-period warrior tale *Heike monogatari* (The Tale of the Heike), which reads: "The blossoms of the sala [sal] trees teach us through their hues that what flourishes must fade."[1]

Śākyamuni is said to have made a final sermon from his deathbed as his disciples assembled there, but Nirvana paintings do not depict that moment; rather, they represent the moment of his death with figures from heaven and earth—bodhisattvas, deities, followers, and even animals—gathered around him. The details of the individual paintings vary, but Buddha's disciples all manifest their shock through expressions of intense anguish. One disciple, Ananda, collapses in agony; another, Anuradha, looks after Ananda; yet another, Mahakasyapa, touches Buddha's feet in veneration, though in actuality he had been in another province at the time of his master's death; and the old man Subhadra, who was Buddha's final disciple, burns himself to death. In contrast, it is customary for the bodhisattvas to be depicted with calm facial expressions, perhaps because they understand that this death is actually the beginning of immortality.

Buddha's Nirvana was first represented symbolically in the form of stupas from about the first century B.C. in Śākyamuni's native India. By the Gandhāran period, however, Nirvana scenes came to depict a recumbent human figure. Typically, these later compositions were simple, with Buddha lying stretched out with his right side down and his head resting on his right arm. A nimbus encircles his head and illuminates his body. His disciples and various other figures surround his bed, which has one sal tree at the right and one at the left. As these motifs spread to China, the compositions grew more diverse, showing variation in the pose of the reclining Buddha, the number of figures in attendance, and the animals, which generally increased in number.

The oldest surviving example of Nirvana art in Japan is a group of earthen sculptures installed at Hōryūji temple in 711. Documentation relating to Nirvana paintings, believed to date as early as the seventh to eighth century, also survives, as do records of a memorial service consecrating a Nirvana painting at Ishiyamadera temple in the early ninth century. The Nehan-e (also Jōraku-e, Nirvana ceremony) service, held in Japan on the anniversary of Buddha's death on the fifteenth day of the second month of the lunar calendar, is believed to be a primary factor in the increase in the production of Nirvana paintings.

The style of Nirvana paintings in Japan from the Heian period onward can be divided into two main groups. The first, thought to imitate Tang-dynasty depictions, is exemplified by Japan's oldest surviving Nirvana painting, popularly known as *Ōtoku Nehan-zu* (Heian period, National Treasure). A wide range of motifs and styles can be seen in this style group, which includes the Tokyo National Museum version (fig. 1) and the Ishiyamadera version (Kamakura period). In this style, a large Buddha figure lies on his back with both arms by his sides at the center of a horizontal composition.

The second style is represented by Nirvana paintings of the Kamakura period believed to be based on the Song-dynasty style. Many of these works are vertical scenes depicting a relatively small Buddha figure with a large number of figures and animals filling the vast space around him. Buddha reclines on his right side with his right arm under his head in a classical pose that can be seen in the earliest Indian Nirvana paintings. The greater number and more realistic depiction of animals, as seen in the late Song-period Nirvana painting housed at Chōfukuji temple in Kyoto, for example, had a profound influence on new Nirvana paintings in Japan, whereas less familiar aspects were modified and given a more Japanese feel.

Thus, Nirvana paintings in Japan developed from two major styles that were introduced from China, but the details were ingeniously arranged to fit Japanese interpretations of the Nirvana sutra and native Japanese customs. Nirvana painting is an extremely important and emotionally significant genre of Buddhist painting, one that evolved as it was transmitted from India to Japan and gave shape to a splendid artistic tradition.

Note

1. Translator's note: From Burton Watson, trans., *The Tales of the Heike*, ed. Haruo Shirane (New York: Columbia University Press, 2006), 9.

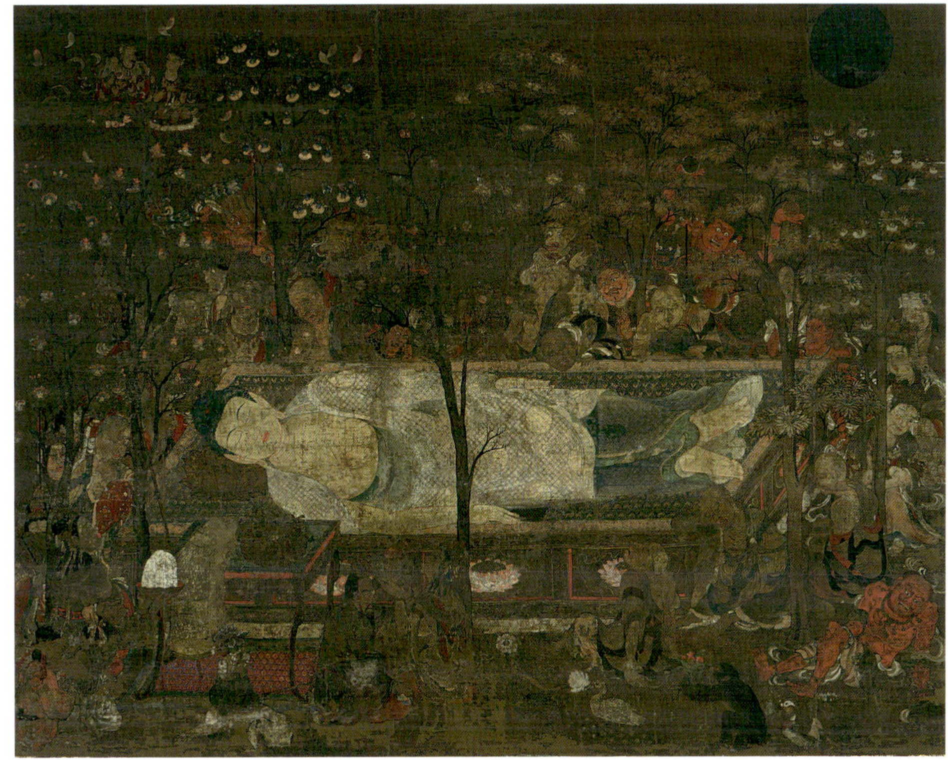

Figure 1
Nirvana Painting,
Important Cultural Property,
Heian period,
Tokyo National Museum.

4.

Nirvana Painting

Kamakura period, 14th century
Hanging scroll, color on silk

75 ⅛ x 47 ⅜ inches (190.7 x 120.4 cm)
Tokyo National Museum

This representation of the deathbed scene of Buddha Śākyamuni belongs to the category of Nirvana paintings from the Kamakura period that shows the influence of Chinese Song- and Yuan-dynasty Nirvana paintings. Buddha lies on a bed positioned at the center of a vertical composition. His pose, lying on his right side with his right arm under his head, originated in Indian Gandhāran art, which was the first to depict Buddha's attainment of Nirvana with a representation of his human form. Disciples and heavenly bodhisattvas surround the bed, individually expressing their grief with quiet intensity.

In the upper section of the painting, two sal trees grow lushly at each of the four sides of the bed, and Buddha's mother, Lady Maya, having heard of his death, descends from heaven. In the lower section, numerous kinds of animals gather around, including a phoenix, elephant, and Chinese lion, as well as an ox and horse, monkey, cat, birds, and even worms and insects. While remaining faithful to the sutra descriptions of Buddha's Nirvana, the artist ingeniously found a way to include animals that would be familiar to the viewer. **S.A.**

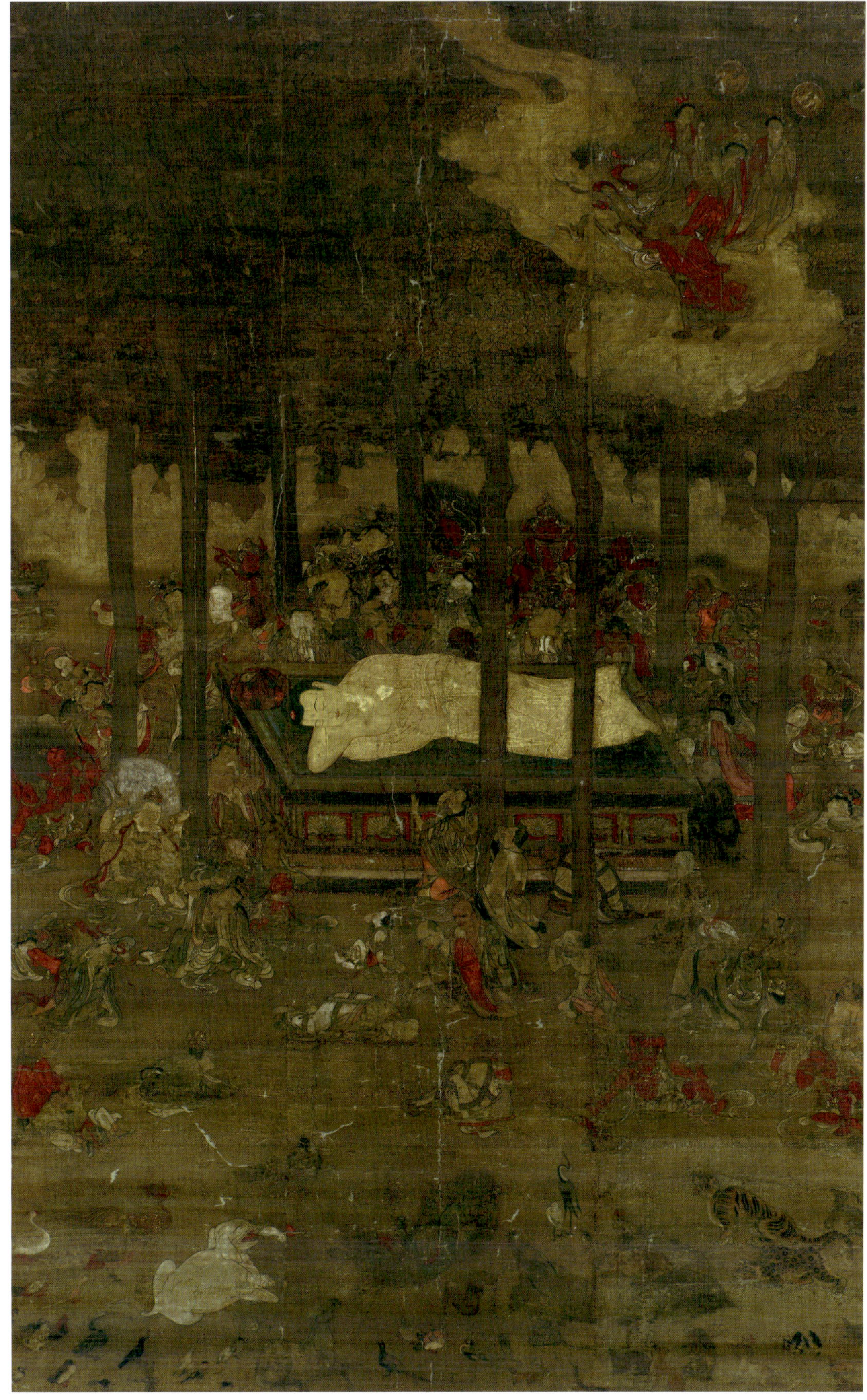

PLATE 4

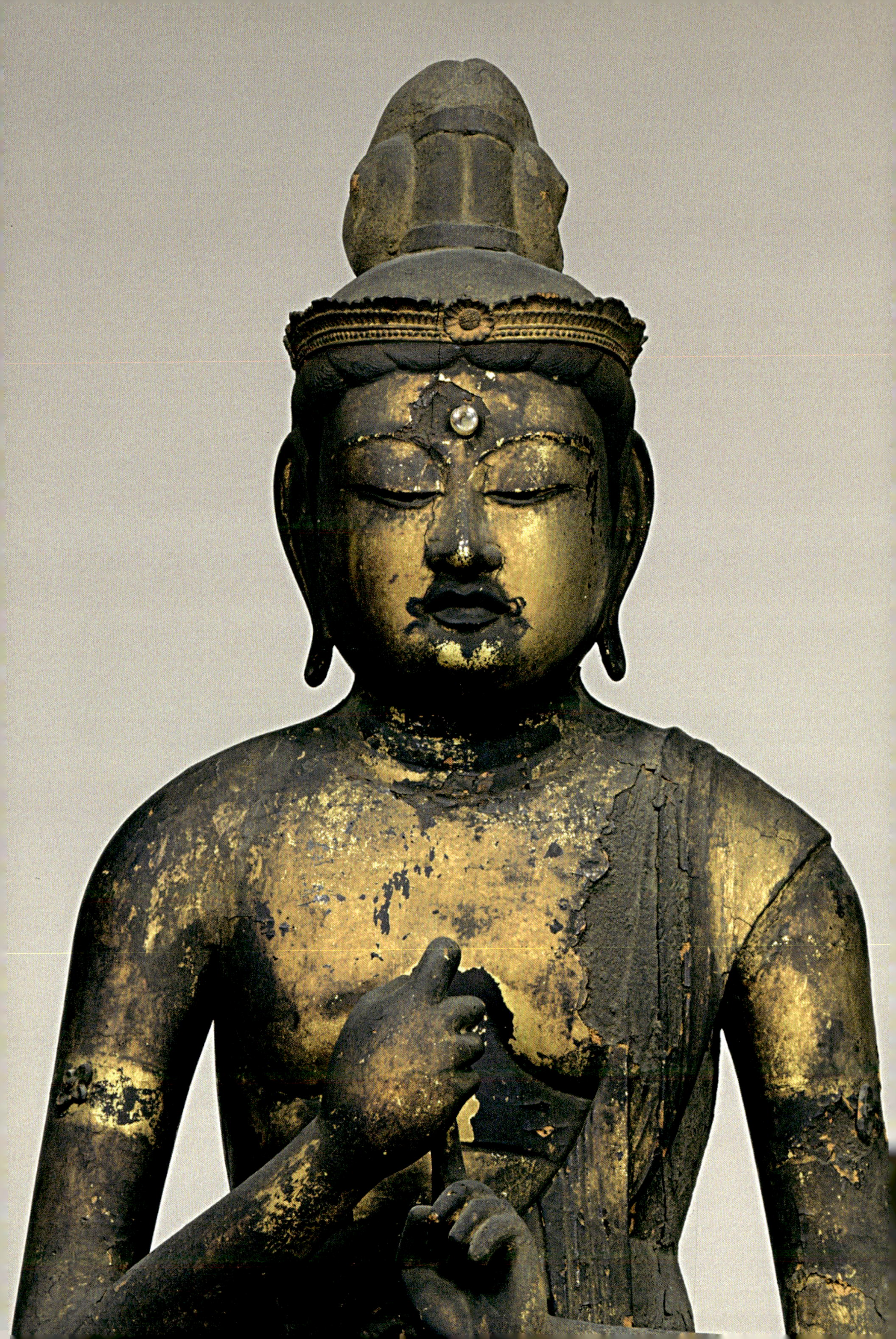

The Sculpture of Dainichi Nyorai

The Sculpture of Dainichi Nyorai

Asami Ryūsuke

Buddhism is a religion that started in India in about the fifth century B.C. and spread to South and Southeast Asia. It was transmitted to Japan from China, passing by way of the Korean Peninsula in the middle of the sixth century. At first, believers of the native Japanese gods opposed the group that was assertively trying to introduce Buddhism (including Chinese and Korean families who had immigrated to Japan), but the followers of Buddhism prevailed, and from the seventh century onward, numerous temples were built and eventually the emperor converted to Buddhism. The native Japanese gods were merged amicably with the Buddhist deities to form an enduring syncretic belief system that is unique to Japan. Until the Meiji period, when laws separating Shinto and Buddhism were enacted, temples and shrines were intimately connected in a synergistic relationship.

Dainichi Nyorai is the principal deity in the Esoteric Buddhist tradition. In the ancient Indian language of Sanskrit, he is known as Mahāvairocana. *Maha* means "great" and *vairocana* means "universally illuminating," as he was considered the center of the universe and a presence equivalent to the Sun. Esoteric Buddhism originated in India and became popular in China in the eighth century. It was brought to Japan by the monk Kūkai (774–835), who had studied in China and had learned there of the Buddhist rituals performed at the Tang court for the peace and prosperity of the nation. Kūkai's request to perform these same rituals in Japan was approved, and the emperor's high regard for such rituals further contributed to the Shingon sect of Esoteric Buddhism founded by Kūkai becoming extremely popular. The Tendai sect founded by Saichō (767–822), who lived during the same period as Kūkai, rivaled Shingon in dispatching monks abroad to study secret transmissions, and consequently, large numbers of Esoteric Buddhist temples were built throughout the Heian period.

These temples enshrined various types of figures besides those of Dainichi Nyorai, some of which had multiple limbs or heads, vestiges of their Indian origins. Esoteric ritual involved incantation and prayer in front of statues of such figures. Believing that it would bring them spiritual rewards, members of the aristocracy sponsored the production of large numbers of Buddhist sculptures and paintings, leading to an increase in the number and variety of such works from the Heian period onward.

Dainichi Nyorai figures are often seated on a lotus pedestal because the lotus was considered sacred for its ability to blossom into beautiful flowers from roots in the mud. These figures have nimbuses at their backs that symbolize their divine nature, but the nimbus of the figure seen in Plate 5 has been lost. Nyorai are enlightened beings (buddhas) commonly depicted with tight spiraling curls, with robes that cover the entire body, and without adornments. However, images of Dainichi Nyorai usually show him with his hair tied up beneath a jeweled crown and with a necklace, armbands, bracelets, and other dazzling items of jewelry. (The original jewelry for the figure seen here has been lost.) Dainichi is a unique example of a nyorai buddha depicted in the manner of a bodhisattva.

There are two types of Dainichi Nyorai, that of the Diamond Realm and that of the Womb Realm. The figure in this catalogue is represented with the index finger of his left hand raised in front of his chest and clasped with his right hand in the "wisdom fist" mudra, which identifies him as Dainichi Nyorai of the Diamond Realm. The Mandala of the Womb Realm depicts how the elements of the universe are born from Dainichi Nyorai and how they expand, whereas the Mandala of the Diamond Realm represents how the entire universe ultimately converges in Dainichi Nyorai. An overwhelming majority of Dainichi Nyorai sculptures represent the Dainichi of the Diamond Realm.

5.

Seated Dainichi Nyorai

Important Cultural Property
Heian period, 11th century
Lacquered wood with gold leaf

Height of figure 36 ¾ inches (93.4 cm);
Height of pedestal 24 ⅛ inches (61.2 cm)
Tokyo National Museum

This is a sculpture of seated Dainichi Nyorai, a central buddha in the Esoteric Buddhist tradition. The figure and the pedestal on which he sits are made from Japanese cypress wood painted with lacquer, over which gold leaf is applied. With the passing of more than eight hundred years, a considerable portion of the gold leaf has come off, but at the time this object was made, the figure would have shone in gold. The face and body appear somewhat slender, and the folds of the skirt wrapping around the lower body are shallow and neatly defined. At the time when this sculpture was made, the Japanese aristocrats had developed their own cultural aesthetic of elegance and restraint. The style of this work reflects such aristocratic taste. **A.R.**

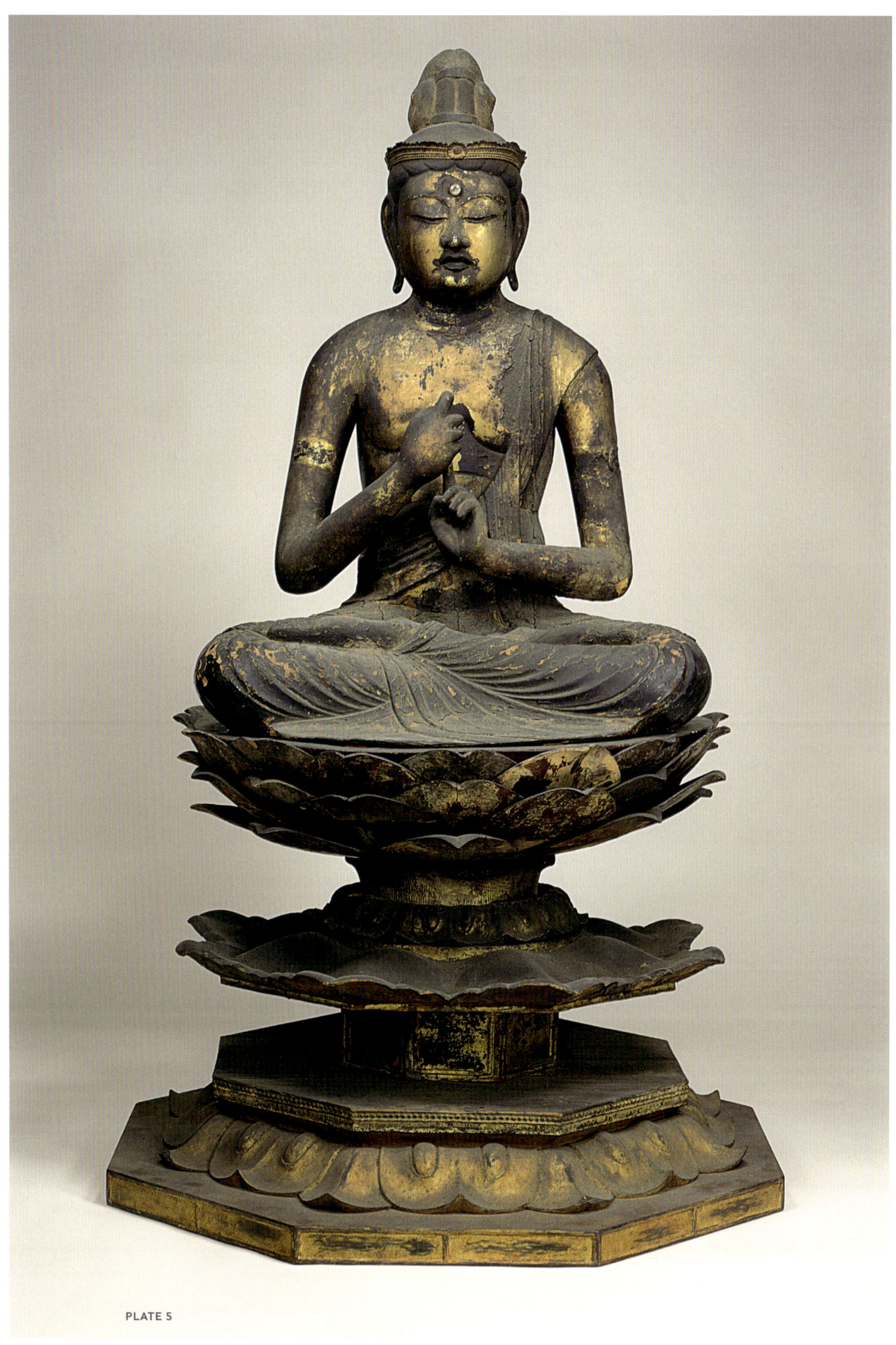

PLATE 5

6.

Standing Zaō Gongen

Kamakura period, 12th–13th century
Bronze

Height: 11¼ inches (28.5 cm)
Tokyo National Museum

Legends say that the syncretic deity Zaō Gongen appeared to the mountain ascetic En no Gyōja (En no Ozunu) while he was in seclusion on Mt. Kinpusen in Yoshino, present-day Nara Prefecture. This belief is affirmed by the unique form of ascetic Buddhism found in Japan known as Shugendō, which promotes spiritual discipline by means of pilgrimages through Mt. Kinpusen and other steep mountains across Japan, or by means of reclusion deep in the mountains. En no Gyōja is considered the founder of Shugendō. Zaō Gongen is a uniquely Japanese deity that does not appear in Buddhist scriptures. Gongen means "avatar" and refers to the temporary manifestation of Buddhist divinities such as Nyorai Buddhas, bodhisattvas, and others in the form of native Japanese Shinto spirits, or *kami*. In other words, Zaō Gongen is both buddha and kami. He emerged with the belief that spread from the Heian period onward that the Buddhist deities transmitted from India via China and Korea and the time-honored kami of Japan were in fact of one body.

In addition to the monumental wooden sculpture standing more than seven meters tall at the head temple of the Shugendō cult on Mt. Kinpusen, icons of Zaō Gongen appear enshrined at mountain temples in the various places where its practitioners conduct their austerities. Like this statue, he is often depicted standing on his left foot with his right foot lifted and his right hand raised overhead, his hair standing on end, and his fangs bared, showing his anger. His right hand holds an esoteric three-pronged vajra club, and his left hand forms the sword mudra (with index and middle fingers extended and the others folded in toward the palm) at his hip, both of which indicate the figure's deep connection to Esoteric Buddhism. The slender and supple body of this figure and the shallowness of the carving are characteristics of Heian-period sculpture of the mid-twelfth century, when sober styles were preferred. However, the dramatic sense of movement is a feature of Kamakura-period sculpture starting at the end of the twelfth century, suggesting that this work was probably made by a conservative sculptor in the Kamakura period. **A.R.**

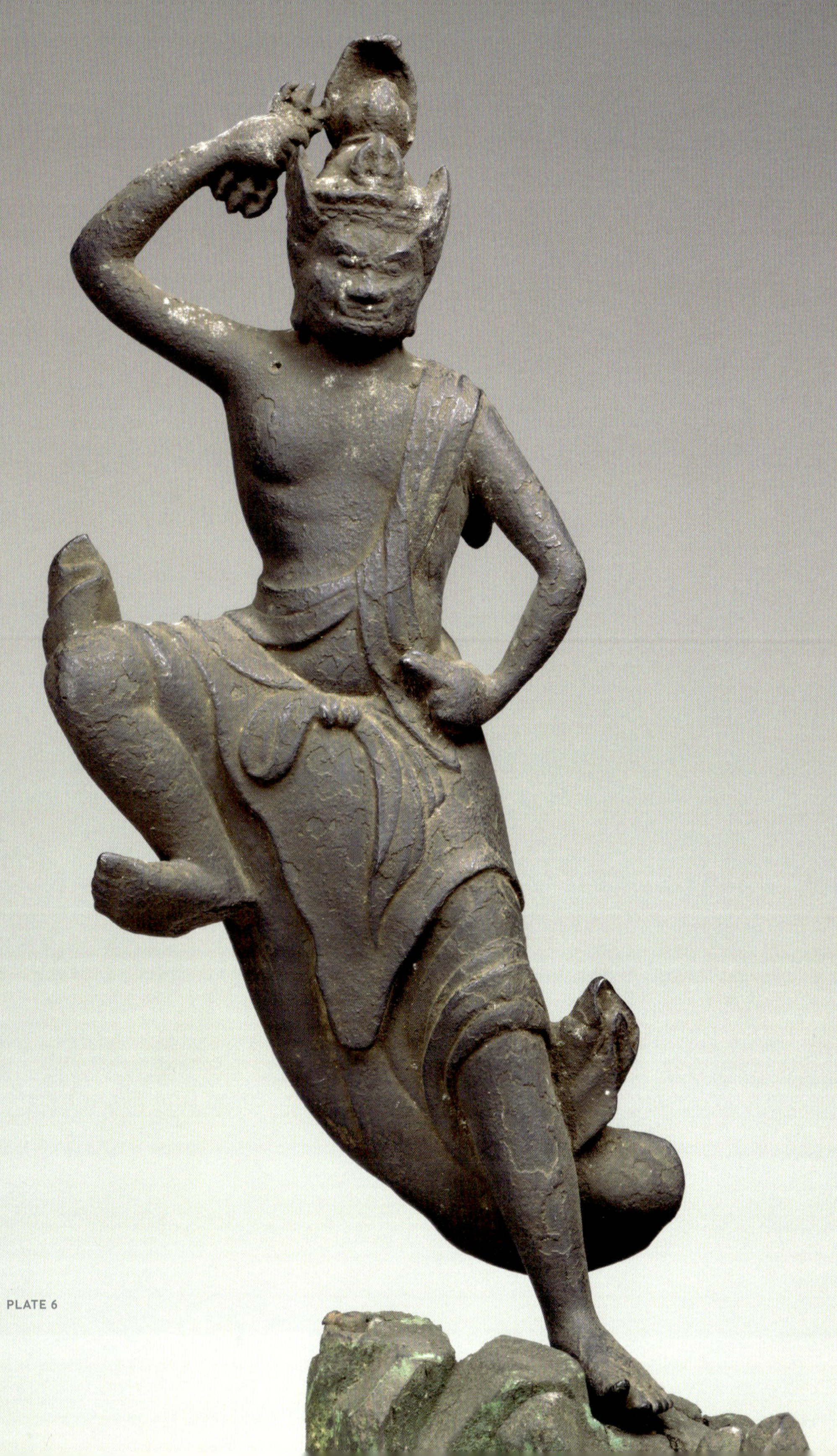

PLATE 6

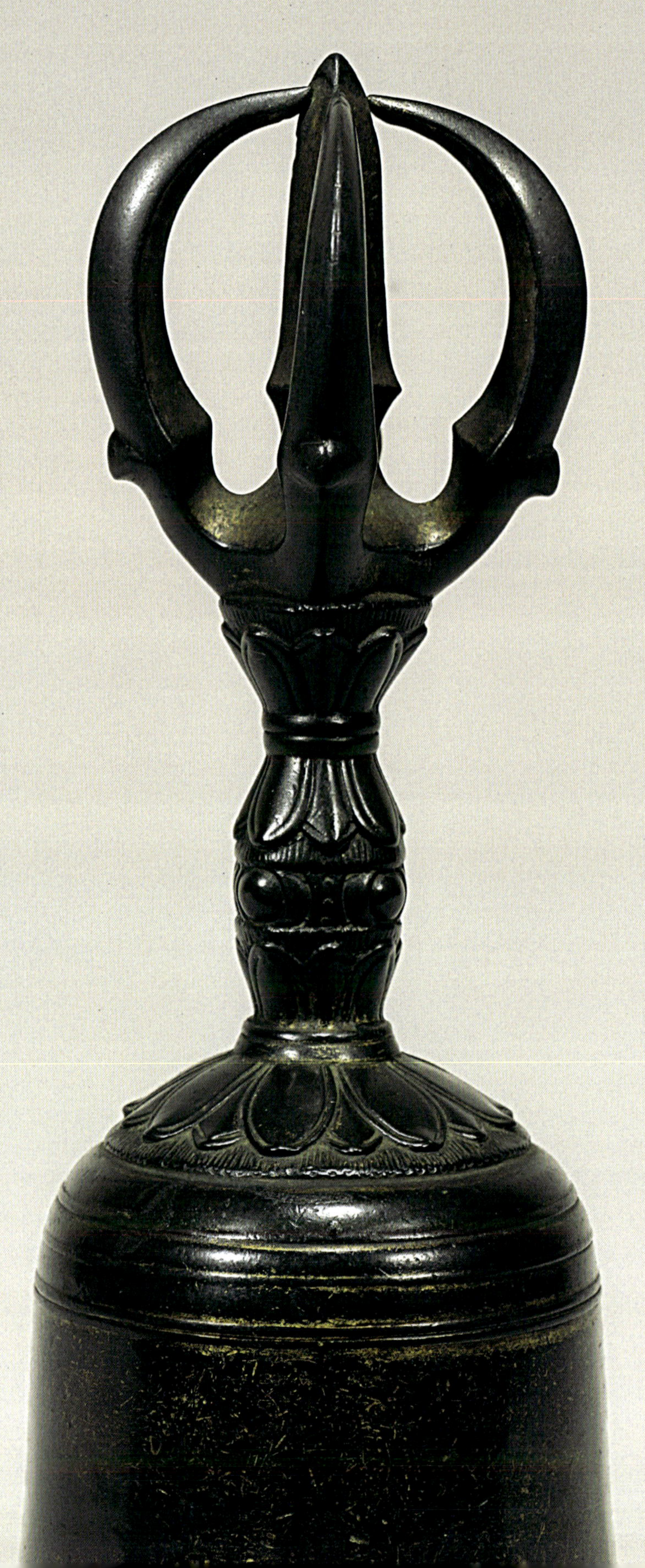

Buddhist Ritual Implements

Buddhist Ritual Implements

Itō Shinji

There are a wide variety of ceremonial implements and vessels used in Buddhist rituals, collectively referred to as "Buddhist ritual implements." This term encompasses all implements and vessels that have some practical function in the practice of Buddhist faith, with the exception of direct objects of worship, such as Buddha sculptures and paintings, and structures such as temples and pagodas, as well as gardens. The materials from which Buddhist implements are made range from metals and wood to bamboo, lacquer, ceramics, textiles, leather, stones and jewels, glass, ivory, and bone. Buddhist implements have practical uses as well as visual and functional beauty, and are generally classified by academics as "decorative arts." However, the extreme diversity of their usage and materials, as well as their role in the shaping of Buddhist faith, makes them a particularly noteworthy genre in the field of decorative arts.

Buddhism originated in the teachings of Buddha (Śākyamuni), who expounded his philosophy from approximately the sixth to the fifth century B.C. As his teachings spread to the various regions of Asia, they mingled at times with the native folk customs of those regions, resulting in a proliferation of belief systems and separate sects that survive to the present day. Today, a number of Buddhist sects exist in Japan, and most Japanese are affiliated with a particular Buddhist sect or temple. The total number of temples in Japan is close to eighty thousand. Although the types of implements used differ slightly among sects, every temple is invariably furnished with some form of altar equipment. Many homes contain objects associated with Buddhist beliefs as well, such as household altars or prayer beads. To accommodate this ongoing need, objects associated with Buddhism continue to be produced in large quantities, and cities such as Tokyo and Kyoto have shopping districts of stores specializing in the sale of Buddhist implements.

The reverence for implements and vessels is believed to have existed in Buddhism since its initial stages. Early Buddhist scriptures use the term "adornment" in reference to the ornamentation of the Buddha's world with numerous treasures, and "memorial service" in reference to offerings of flowers, incense, and candles with food and drink. These writings also suggest that vessels of various kinds were developed specifically to be used for such offerings. Additionally, these scriptures contain detailed provisions for the types of accoutrements that monks should wear. Buddhism arrived in Japan in the sixth century in the form of doctrine and Buddhist icons that served as objects of worship, and was accompanied by a great number of imported implements, which served as models for domestic production. Over time, the complex separation of Buddhism into a multitude of different sects in Japan led to a surge in the production of implements and a diversification of the types and styles of items being produced.

Although the strict classification of Buddhist implements is no simple task, considering the wide range of items that fall under that term, these objects are generally grouped by function into the following basic categories:

- **adornments:** items that decorate Buddhist icons and the interior and exterior spaces of buildings, such as altars, miniature shrines, canopies, banners, and low tables;
- **offering implements:** items used when presenting offerings to deities, such as incense burners, lanterns, flower vases, and vessels for food and drink;
- **ceremonial implements:** items used for conducting ritual observances, such as accoutrements for esoteric rituals, musical instruments, and equipment for Buddhist rites; and
- **monks' accoutrements:** items worn or carried by monks, such as *kesa* robes, prayer beads, and water ewers.

This catalogue presents various ritual implements that are used specifically in the Esoteric Buddhist tradition. Esoteric Buddhism is a belief system that emerged in India during the final stages of the development of early Buddhist faith and is characterized by its convergence with native folk customs and with the religious traditions of Brahmanism and Hinduism. As Esoteric Buddhism developed, it grew to focus more explicitly on averting misfortune and seeking blessings in the current life, resulting in a rapid increase in the number of deified figures, each of whom offered specific benefits. Furthermore, the procedures for worshipping individual deities came to be minutely prescribed and heavily infused with ritual. Esoteric altar implements were indispensable items in conducting these ceremonies. The pointed shape of implements such as the vajra club and crossed vajra symbolizes the rejection of worldly desires and evil spirits and alludes to the origins of these objects in ancient Indian weaponry. The vajra bell purifies space with its clear ring and serves to awaken dormant piety within the devotee. Various types of vessels are also used to make offerings of incense, flowers, candles, food, and drink to Buddha. These vessels are systematically arranged on top of the altar in a temple's main hall in accordance with specific ordinances, and the dazzling radiance emitted by the many gilt-bronze pieces contributes to the unique ambience of the space. These various accoutrements could be classified under the aforementioned categories of adornments and offering implements. However, when used specifically for esoteric ritual, they are generally collectively known as esoteric ritual implements.

In the early ninth century, Kūkai and other monks traveled to Tang China with a strong desire to learn the secret transmissions of Esoteric Buddhism. They brought back to Japan a great many sutra texts, Buddhist paintings, and esoteric ritual implements to accompany the systematized doctrine. With the prosperity of Esoteric Buddhism throughout the Heian period (ninth through twelfth century), esoteric ritual implements also came to be produced domestically in great numbers. Their unique shapes, purposes, and arrangement according to strict specifications convey a mysterious radiance that gives esoteric ritual implements a splendor that is distinctive among Buddhist altar goods.

7. [PICTURED ON FOLLOWING PAGES]

Kasha (Incense Burner) and Set of Six Ritual Bowls

Kamakura period, 13th–14th century
Gilt bronze

Kasha: height 4 ⅝ inches (11.7 cm);
burner: height 2 ⅛ inches (5.4 cm),
diameter 4 ¾ inches (11.9 cm),
height of lid 2 ⅝ inches (6.5 cm),
diameter of lid 4 ½ inches (11.4 cm)

Six ritual bowls: height 1 ¾ inches (4.2 cm),
diameter of mouth 3 ⅛–3 ¼ inches (8–8.1 cm),
height of base 1 ⅝ inches (4.1 cm),
height of bowls ⅛ inch (2.2–2.3 cm),
diameter of bowls 3–3 ⅛ inches (7.6–7.8 cm),
height of bowl bases ⅝–⅛ inches (1.6–1.8 cm),
diameter of bowl bases 2 ⅛–2 ⅜ inches (5.4–6.1 cm)
Tokyo National Museum

These objects are ceremonial implements that are placed on a Buddhist altar during esoteric rituals. They are usually arranged as a complete set, with the incense burner at the center and three small bowls, each with a dish under it, positioned in a straight line at either side. Alternatively, four sets may be arranged along the four outer edges of the square altar or just a single set placed along the front edge. The number of sets used depends on the type of ritual being performed.

The incense burner consists of a tripodal brazier pot with a lid. The six bowls are usually filled with purified water, incense, or flower petals, but the specific items differ among the esoteric sects. In some cases, all six are filled with leaves. In addition to decorating the altar, these implements also function as dedicatory vessels for making offerings to Buddha. Fewer vessels were used when Esoteric Buddhism was first brought to Japan in the ninth century. The tradition of using a set of six bowls was established in about the twelfth century.

These pieces were made from cast bronze, and after the exterior was ground on a wheel to refine the shape, gold plating was applied to the surface. The consistency of style demonstrates that the individual pieces were not gathered at random but were made intentionally as a set. The rather heavy construction, the tall lid of the incense burner, the short, stout feet, and the comparatively tall foot ring on the bottoms of the six bowls are recognizable characteristics of early to mid-fourteenth-century style. These objects' consistent form and robust modeling, and their slightly blunt impression, are typical of fourteenth-century Japanese metalwork. I.S.

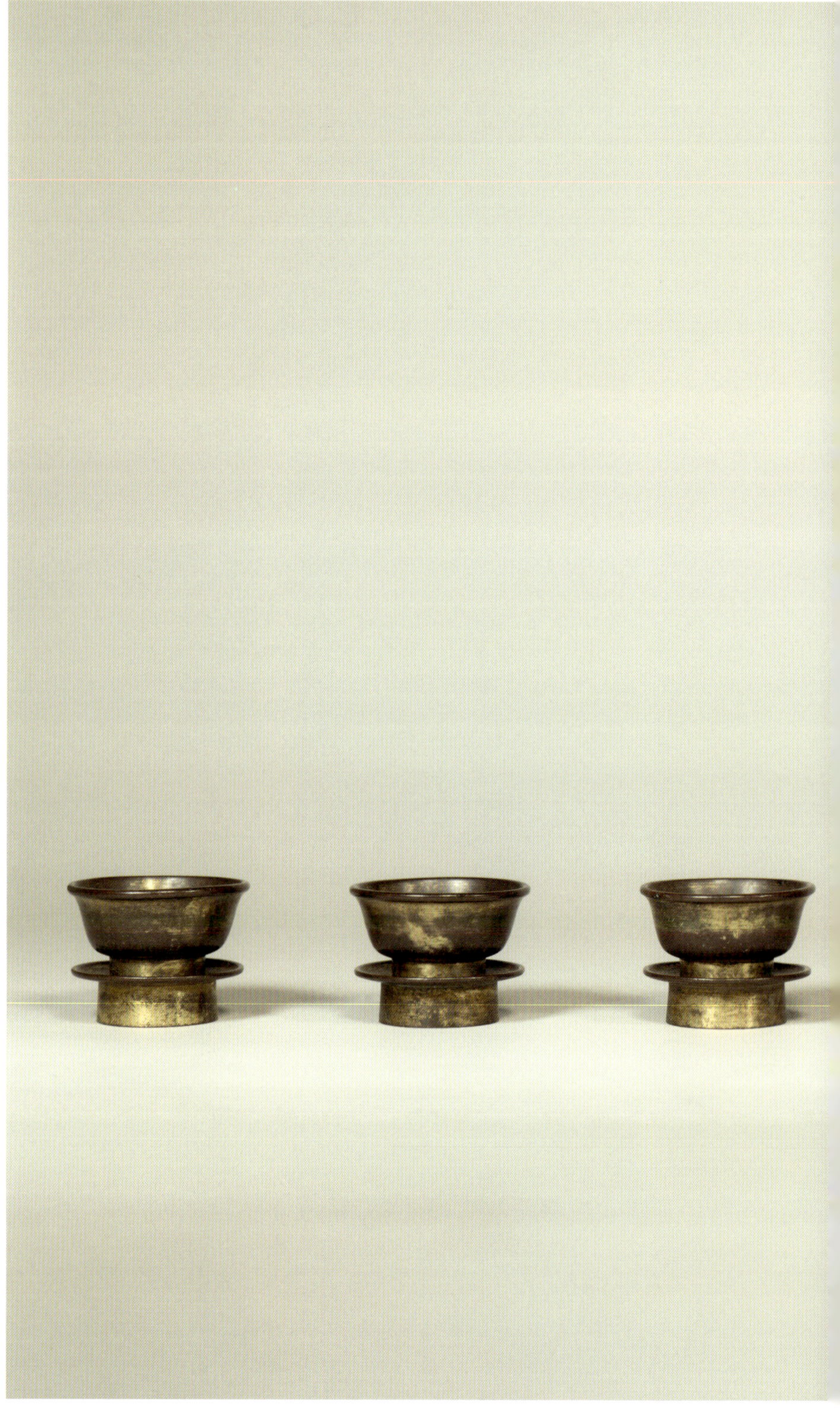

PLATE 7

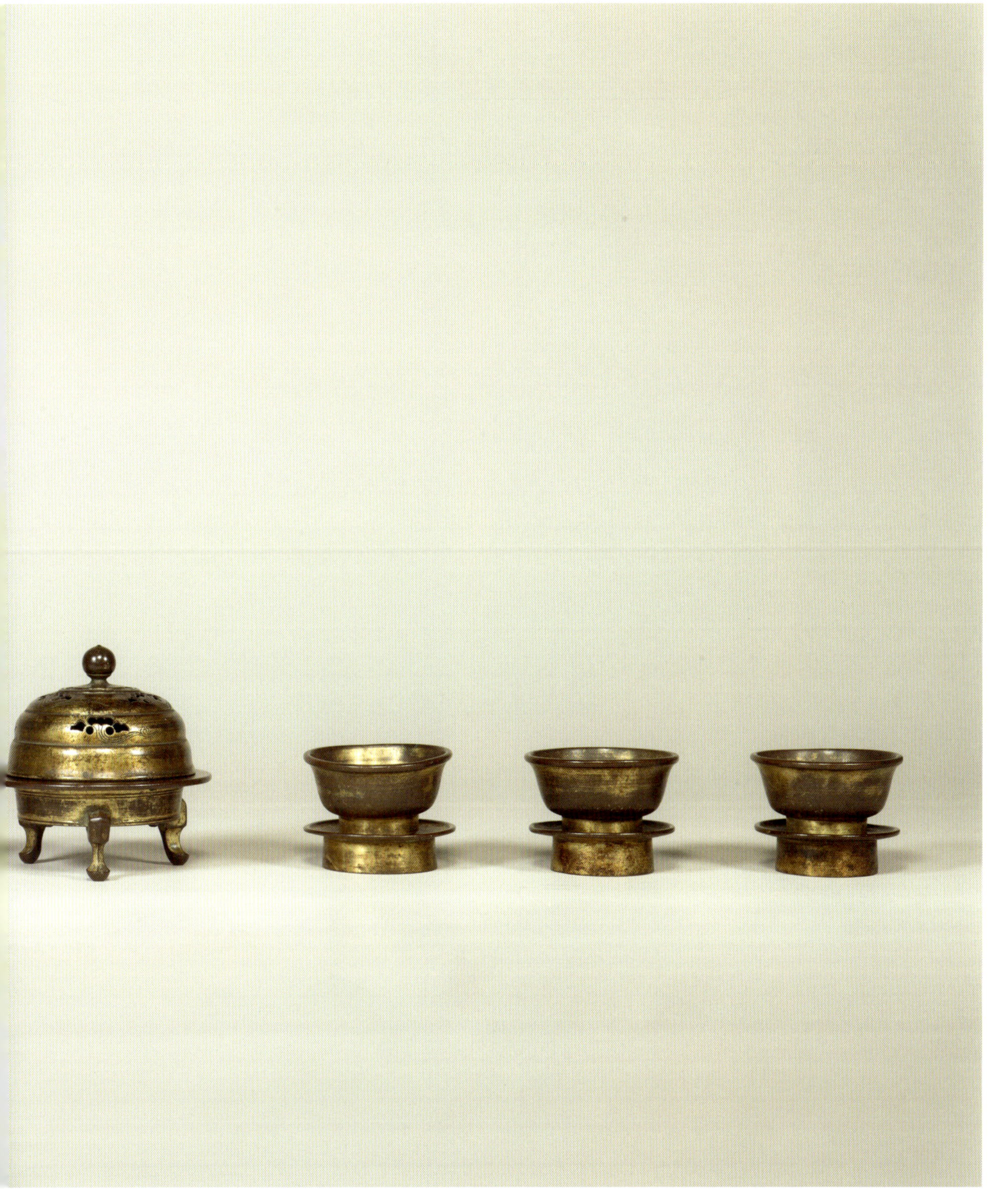

8.

Five-pronged Vajra Bell

Heian period, 12th century
Gilt bronze

Height 6 ½ inches (16.6 cm); diameter of mouth 2 ⅞ inches (7.4 cm)
Tokyo National Museum

The five-pronged vajra bell combines an upper section with five inwardly curving points, called a vajra, and a lower section in the shape of a bell. Several other types of bells with handles fashioned in the shape of vajras exist, like the one pictured here, and these are known collectively as vajra bells. Of these, the five-pronged bell is one of the most popular altar implements and is used in most esoteric rituals, where it serves symbolically to pacify the altar space and functionally to mark critical junctures in the ritual when rung by a priest. At Kyōōgokokuji temple in Kyoto, a five-pronged vajra bell brought to Japan from China in the ninth century by the Esoteric Buddhist monk Kūkai still survives.

The vajra bell is given an important role in esoteric practice. Purifying the ritual space, it offers a pure sound to the Buddhist deities while awakening the dormant piety within those who hear it. The clear, serene sound of the bell is also extremely effective in elevating the mystical ambiance of the rituals.

Made from gilt bronze, the tines of this five-pronged vajra handle, which resemble ox horns, are dynamically curved, and the pointed tips are sharply tapered. On the bell portion, the shoulder line is gently rounded, and the line from the body to the bell opening presents a natural curve. The five-pronged vajra portion is only slightly longer than that of the bell. These characteristics indicate a twelfth-century Heian-period style. In vajra bells made from the thirteenth century onward, the shoulders tend to become broader, the mouth of the bell to open wider, and the vajra portion to be significantly longer than the bell. **I.S.**

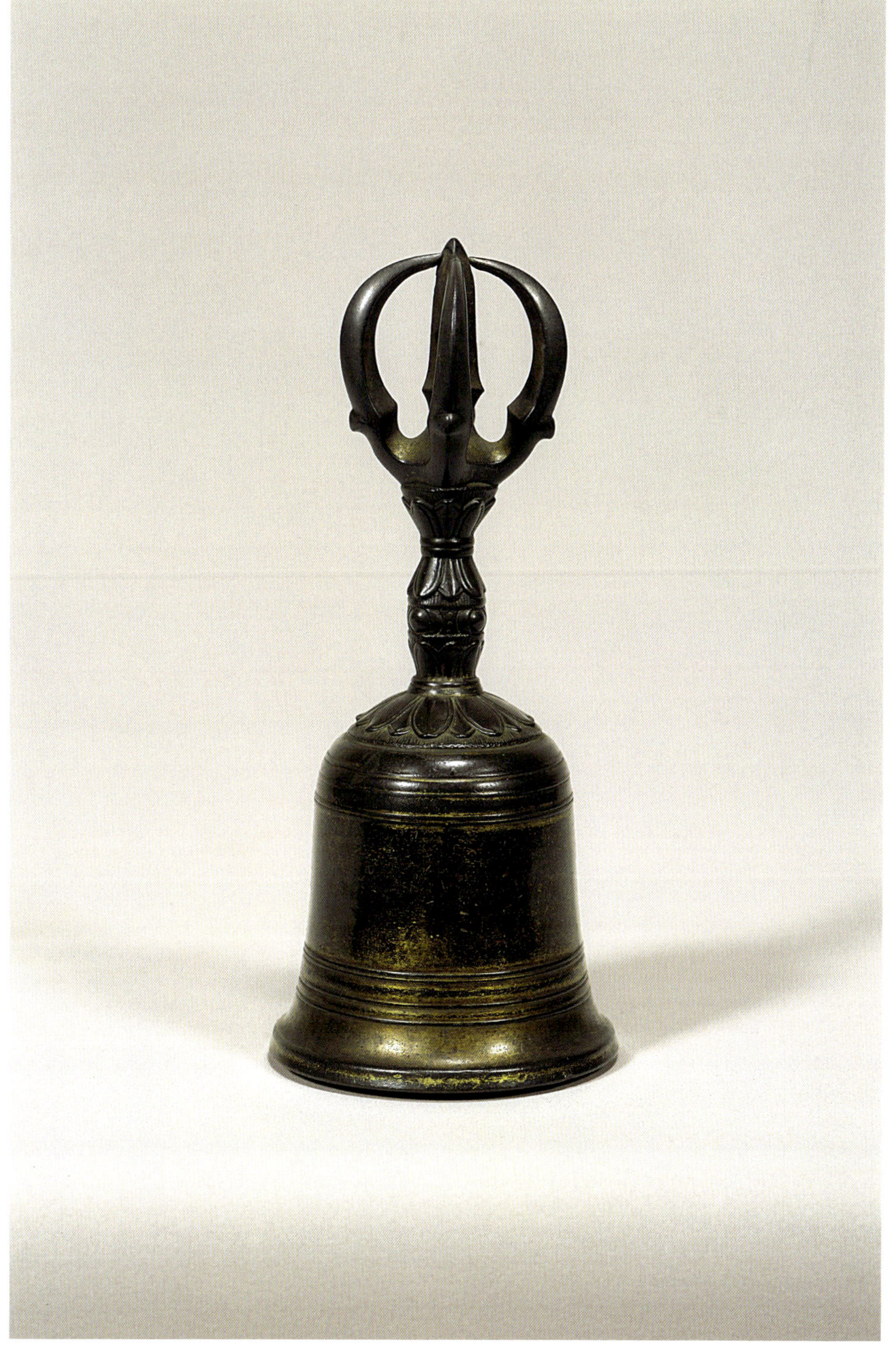

PLATE 8

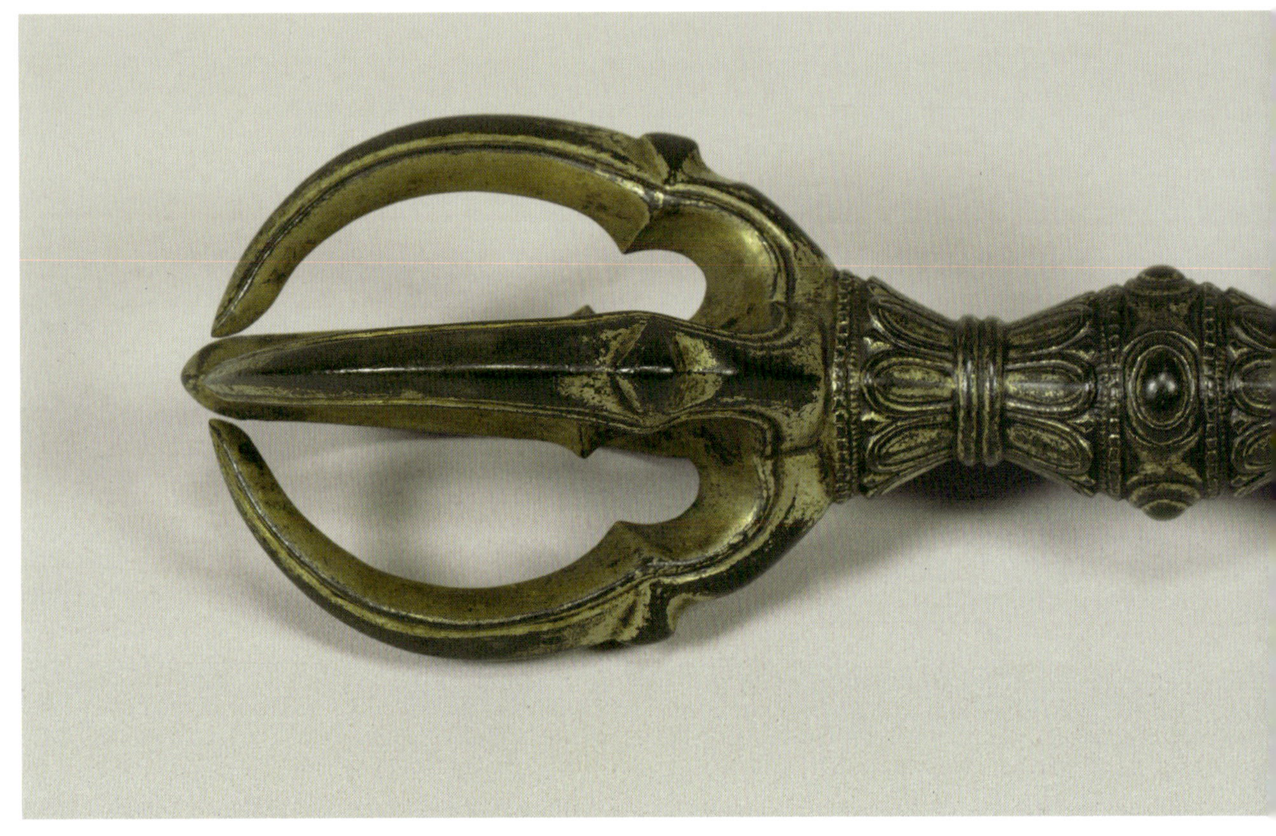

9.

Five-pronged Vajra Club

Kamakura period, 13th century
Gilt bronze

Length 7 inches (17.9 cm)
Tokyo National Museum

This object is called a five-pronged double vajra because of the five pointed protuberances on each end. Similar objects with differing numbers of protuberances are known variously as "single-pronged clubs," "three-pronged clubs," or "nine-pronged clubs," and are collectively referred to as vajra clubs. The sharp tips are vestiges of ancient Indian weapons. As mentioned also in the preceding essay, Esoteric Buddhism incorporated aspects of the native Indian religions of Brahmanism and Hinduism during the developmental stage of Buddhism. However, the esoteric tradition adopted such objects for use as altar implements, not because of their practical function as weapons but ultimately for their specific spiritual implications—their sharp points were symbolically associated with the quelling of worldly desires and evil spirits. The vajra is the implement that best embodies the principles of esoteric ritual, and as a motif, it is found repeatedly in bells and other ritual implements.

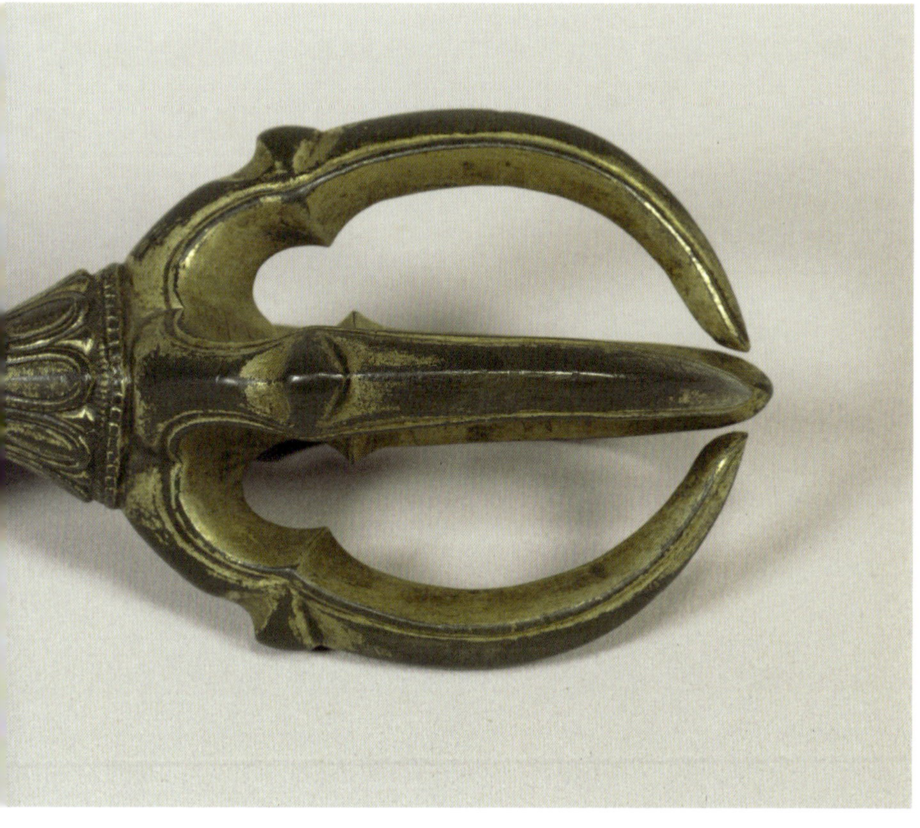

PLATE 9

The five-pronged vajra, like the five-pronged vajra bell (Plate 8), is considered particularly important among the various types of vajras, and it graces the altar in almost all esoteric rituals. Like the five-pronged vajra bell, it is placed on the altar and at certain critical junctures in the rites the priest raises it as he chants mantras.

This particular five-pronged vajra shows visible partial abrasion of the gold plating, perhaps due to frequent usage. The overall shape is well balanced, and the curve of the prongs is somewhat gentle, while the pointed tips have lost some of their sharpness. These details indicate that it was made in the thirteenth century. I.S.

10.

Bell with Handle in the Shape of a Stupa

Kamakura period, 13th century
Gilt bronze

Height 6 ½ inches (21 cm); diameter of mouth 2 ⅞ inches (8 cm)
Tokyo National Museum

This vajra bell features a stupa-shaped upper section. Stupas were reliquaries for enshrining Buddha's relics. In India after Buddha died, his body was cremated and his remains distributed among several burial sites by the people who sought to experience his compassion. To house and worship his relics, eight monumental stupas were built. In the third century B.C., King Ashoka of the Maurya dynasty is said to have removed the relics from seven of these stupas and to have distributed them among eighty-four thousand stupas that he had built throughout India. This custom of relic worship spread with Buddhism to distant regions as well. These objects, called Buddha's relics, were not actual bones in many cases but small pieces of crystal and other precious stones that symbolized Buddha's remains and were commonly consecrated in metal, crystal, or glass containers and housed in stupas. In Japan, stupas were built promptly upon the arrival of Buddhism in the sixth century. Before long, it became popular practice to create small-scale stupas to be used as reliquaries. It is believed that the stupa motif was adopted for use on the vajra bell because of the fervent worship of Buddha's relics inherent in Esoteric Buddhist practice. Documentary records report that Kūkai brought a Chinese stupa bell to Japan from China in the ninth century, but no examples of such bells survive from before the twelfth century. The stupa portion of the bell seen here is removable. Although it is currently empty, it probably once held Buddha's relics. **I.S.**

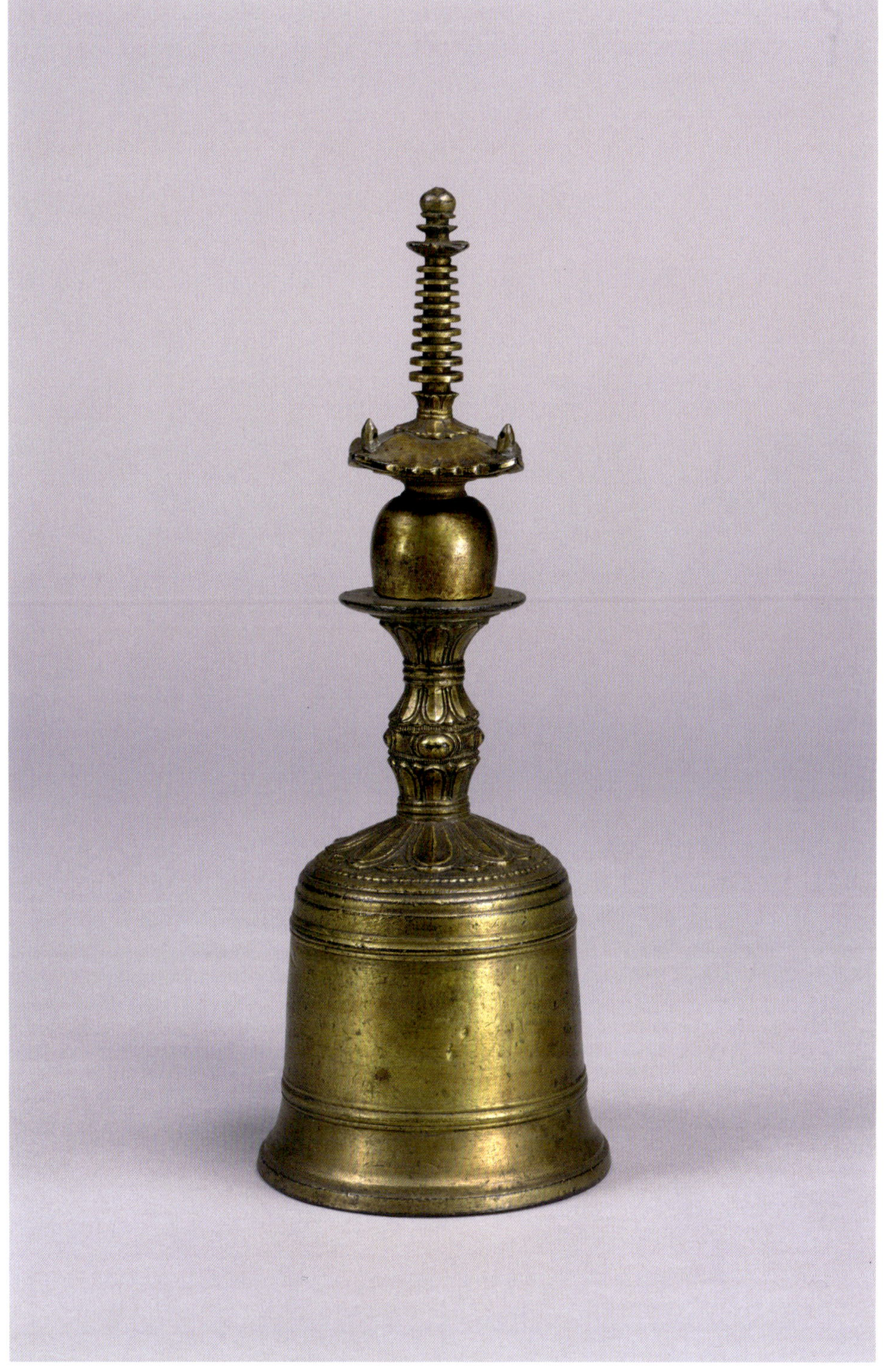

PLATE 10

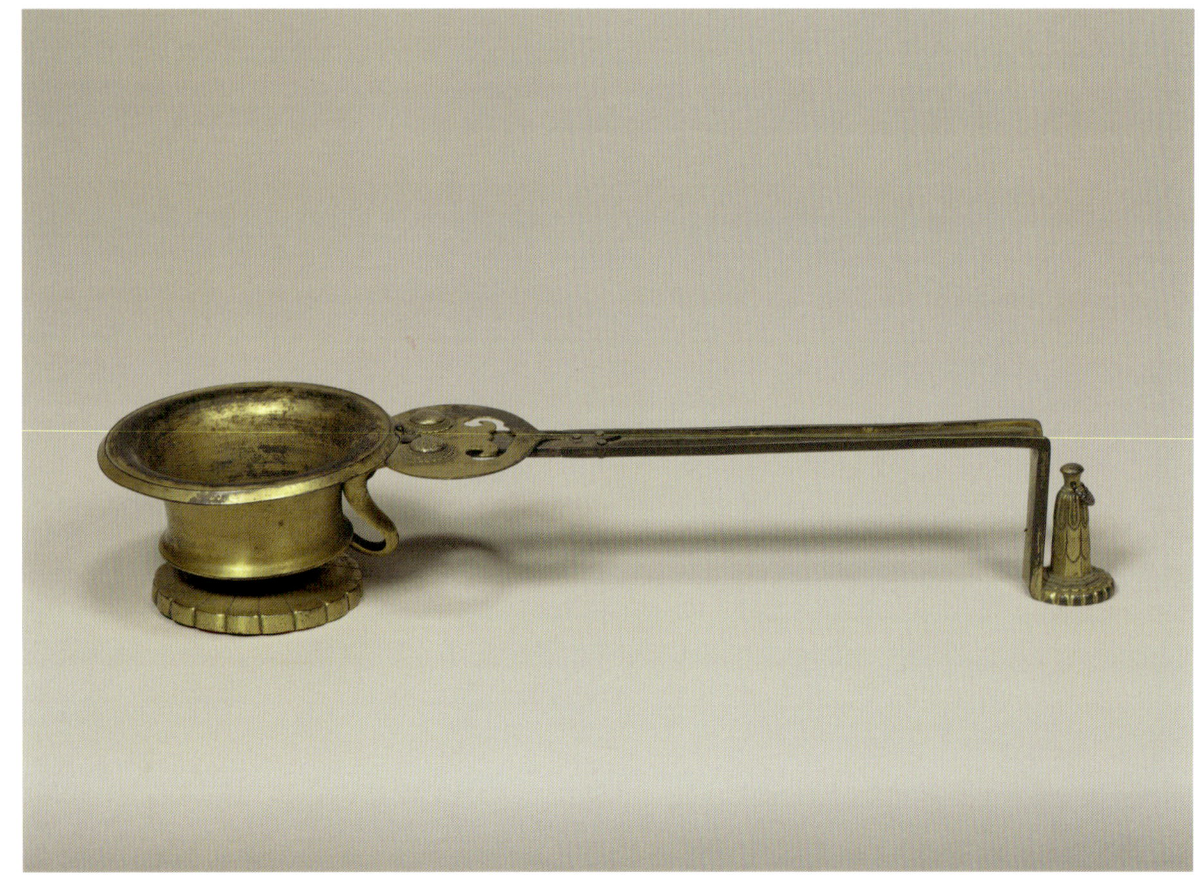

PLATE 11

11.

Incense Burner with Handle

Heian period, 12th century
Gilt bronze

Length 14 ⅛ inches (35.8 cm); diameter of burner cup 4 ¼ inches (10.6 cm)
Tokyo National Museum

This long-handled incense burner consists of a flat base and a flared cup for incense with a long handle. The end of the handle is bent at a right angle, giving the incense burner stability when it is set down. In addition, an ornamental weight is attached at the tip of the handle to counter the weight of the cup when it is carried. These balance weights were generally made in the shape of either a water jug or a Chinese lion.

Handled censers have a long history, and examples of Buddha figures holding them can be seen in art as early as Gandhāran sculpture. They were introduced to Japan with the transmission of Buddhism, and surviving examples, as well as painted images of them being used, indicate that they were produced abundantly by the seventh century. These censers were implements used in ritual offerings of incense to Buddhist images, and were objects that monks were supposed to keep among their possessions.

This work, with a water-jug-shaped weight, most likely had a lid that is now lost. Because the shape of this type of incense burner hardly changed from the seventh century onward, the date for this object is difficult to determine. However, comparisons to other known works indicate that it was probably made in the twelfth century.

As the Gandhāran example demonstrates, long-handled incense burners were already widely used in Buddhist practice even before the emergence of Esoteric Buddhism; however, it should be noted that this particular altar item also appears in most rituals of Esoteric Buddhism. **I.S.**

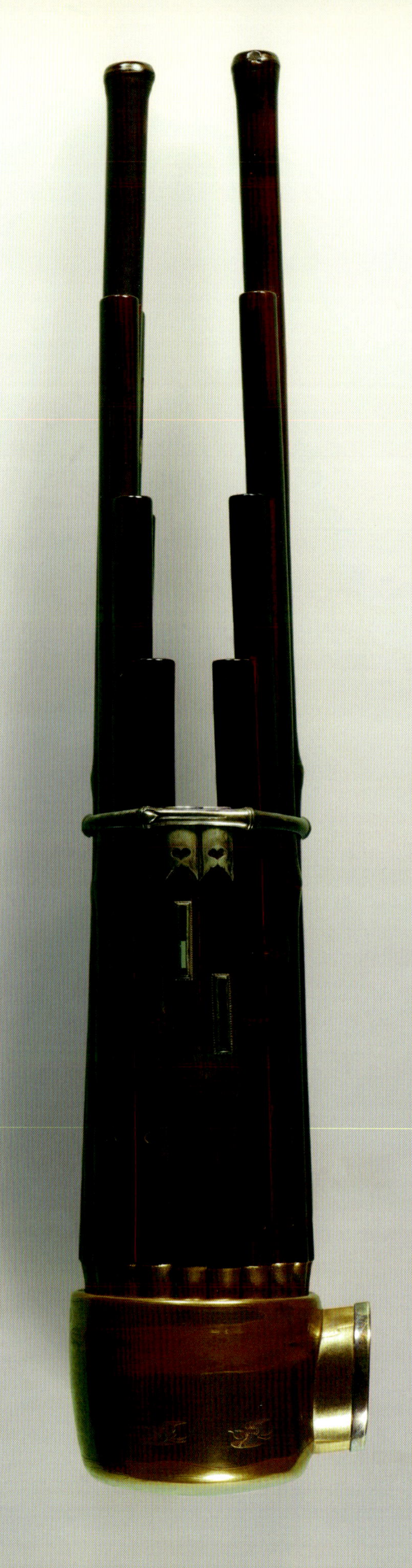

Musical Instruments and the Lacquer Arts Tradition

Musical Instruments and the Lacquer Arts Tradition

Takeuchi Namiko

To the Japanese, musical instruments were not mere tools. Noteworthy instruments that emerged throughout the ages, boasting either some distinctive pedigree or exceptional tonal quality, were carefully stored in lavishly ornate silk sacks or cases decorated in intricate lacquer designs. In addition, individual instruments were frequently given unique poetic names, and imagery associated with those names often appeared in the designs adorning the instrument or case in which it was stored. The techniques used to decorate these pieces included *maki-e*, in which gold dust is sprinkled over designs painted in lacquer; *raden*, in which pieces of mother-of-pearl are cut to form designs and are inlaid into the surface; and *chōshitsu*, in which designs are carved into multiple overlapping layers of lacquer. The variety of lacquer techniques used to decorate musical instruments is noteworthy, and the number of beautifully adorned musical instruments that were produced in Japan further demonstrates the depth of the premodern Japanese appreciation of musical instruments as works of art.

The richness of the lacquer decorations found on various ancient musical instruments that have survived to the present day embodies the admiration and pleasure that Japanese people felt for these instruments. The pieces shown in this catalogue offer a glimpse of the extent to which these musical instruments were enjoyed by the people who used them.

A number of musical instruments lavishly decorated with mother-of-pearl and tortoiseshell inlay—including *koto* (Japanese zithers), *genkan* (Chinese lutes), *biwa* (Japanese lutes), and *kugo* (Chinese harps)—appear among the Shōsōin Treasures, a collection of artifacts representing the finest examples of decorative art objects of the Nara period (eighth century). The exceptional ornamentation of these pieces distinguishes them even among the other treasured artifacts in the Shōsōin collection. In Japan, the blending and convergence of dance and music from China, the Korean Peninsula, and other regions during the Nara period constituted the origins of *gagaku*, a form of classical court music that was to become the root of all traditional Japanese music. The ensuing Heian period brought increased adaptation to Japanese customs, and gagaku was extensively reformed, resulting in a uniquely Japanese style of music. Gagaku was enthusiastically adopted for use at court functions and was also widely performed on a smaller scale in the form of chamber music, which became a favorite amusement for the court aristocrats. As a result of this close association with the imperial court, gagaku gradually went into decline from the Kamakura period onward when the samurai class came to power.

After a prolonged period of peace in the Edo period, gagaku experienced a revival among the samurai classes and at temples and shrines. The shogunate established an official system of musicians, and gagaku became a part of religious festivals and other ceremonies. Also in the Edo period, collecting ancient gagaku instruments came into vogue among upper-class warrior families, who acquired renowned musical instruments that had been passed down through temples and shrines, aristocratic families, and families of musicians. This trend further cultivated the aforementioned appreciation and veneration of musical instruments.

The storage cases for *ryūteki* (dragon flutes), *komabue* (Korean flutes), *hichiriki* (double-reed flutes), and other instruments were often decorated with elaborate maki-e compositions, some of which were designed by famous maki-e artists. The reed instrument known as the *shō* is often decorated with detailed maki-e designs painted on the section called the *kashira* (head or bowl), which includes the mouthpiece. Before being played, the bowl of the shō was heated over a charcoal fire in order to dry the inside, which often caused damage to this part of the instrument. As a result, many shō have bowls that were remade in the Edo period, though their bamboo tubes might be much older. Similarly, the various flutes also often show evidence of later restoration, such as the rewrapping of the bark strips that decorate the outside or the brilliant edging of the mouthpiece or finger holes in red lacquer. Fundamentally, musical instruments are functional objects that inevitably sustain some damage through use. The Japanese tradition of restoring and repairing the instruments and decorations allowed them to be used over a very long time and to be passed down to later generations.

Such repairs were not limited to musical instruments. Lacquer was commonly used to repair virtually any lacquered object that had peeled or chipped, thus extending its useful life. Furthermore, lacquer was used widely both as an adhesive as well as a coating for repairing various wood and ceramic objects and all types of vessels. In the context of a culture that valued old things and placed great importance on tradition, the all-purpose natural substance of lacquer was an indispensable material due to its bonding strength, resistance to both acid and alkaline environments, and its waterproof qualities.

12.

Shō (mouth-organ) called "Mura-chidori"

By Sono Hironaga
Edo period, dated 1690
Bamboo and lacquered wood with maki-e sprinkled gold design bearing inscriptions identifying artist and date

Length 18 inches (45.8 cm)
Tokyo National Museum

The *shō* is a musical instrument that was brought to Japan from China. It is also called a *hōshō* because the overall shape resembles a standing mythical firebird (*hō-ō*) with upraised wings. The shō that entered Japan from China in the Nara period had an additional pipelike mouthpiece, but in Japan the shape evolved so that the instrument was played by blowing into it directly. On the Japanese shō, the main body of the instrument (the round piece that includes the mouth hole) is called the *kashira* (or *hō*). Seventeen thin bamboo pipes are inserted at the top of the kashira. Sound is produced by inhaling and exhaling into the mouth hole and by covering and uncovering the holes at the bases of each of the bamboo pipes. Different fingering combinations allow for a total of eleven different chords.

In keeping with its name, *"Mura-chidori"* (Flock of Plovers), this shō bears motifs of plovers flying about the water's edge painted on the main body. *Maki-e* designs in powders of gold, silver, and a gold-silver alloy that presents a bluish hue express the plovers in minute detail, down to the feathers, eyes, and beaks. The overall surface of the body is prepared with a gold ground, and the swirling lines of the water have a delicate effect, creating an extravagant yet refined design. One of the bamboo pipes bears an inscription dating the work to the year 1690 and identifying the maker as Sono Hironaga, of the Uzumasa clan, who was affiliated with the department of court music at Shitennōji temple in Osaka. This instrument is a rare and important example of a shō whose maker and date of production are clearly known. **T.N.**

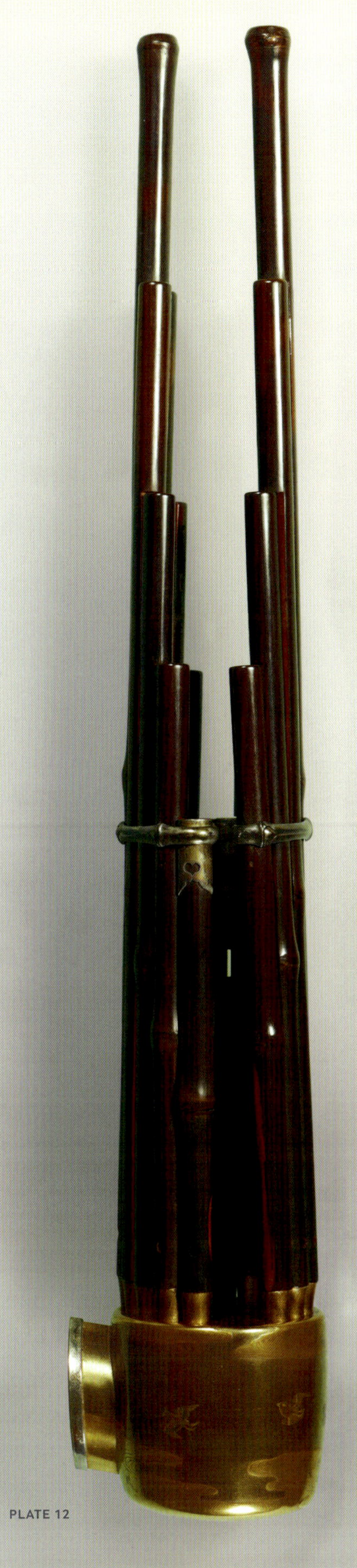

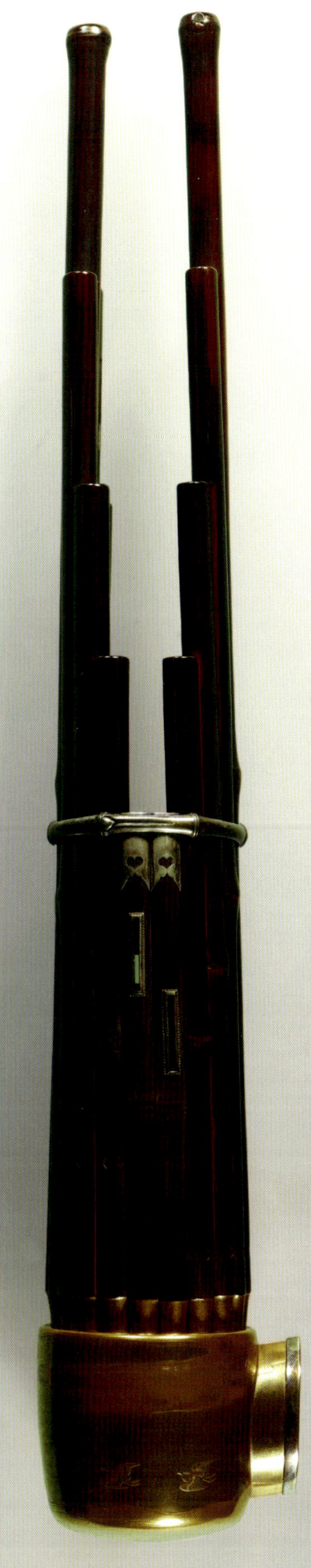

PLATE 12

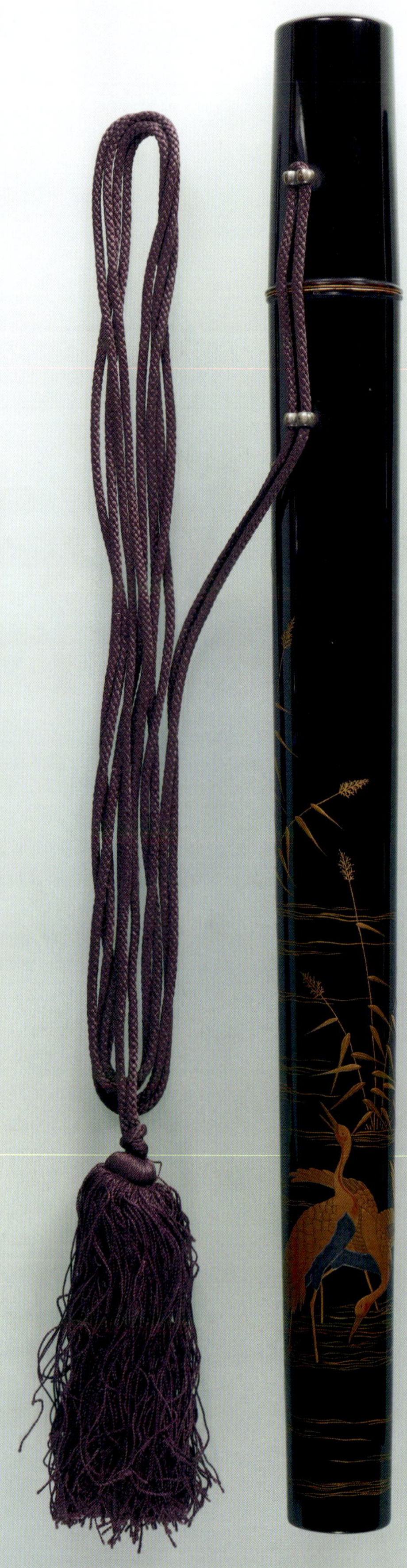

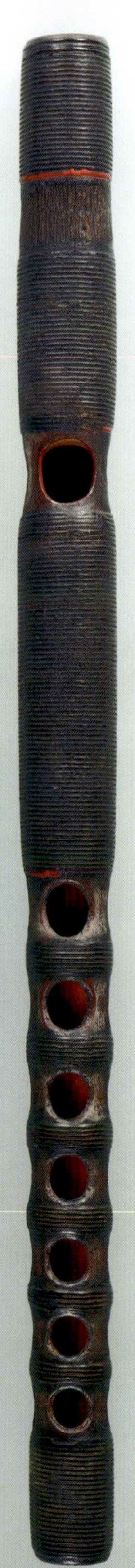

PLATE 13

13.

Ryūteki (dragon flute) called "Ashitazu"

Muromachi period, 15th century
Bamboo wrapped with black lacquered bark strips

Length 15 ¾ inches (40 cm)
Tokyo National Museum

The *ryūteki* flute came from China and, together with the *shō* and *hichiriki*, was used for performing the type of gagaku music known as *tōgaku* or Tang-style pieces. It had a wider register than these other instruments, encompassing both low and high tones. Its timbre was thought to suggest the voice of the dragon (*ryū*), hence the name ryūteki (literally "dragon flute"). The ryūteki is a transverse bamboo flute with seven finger holes. With the exception of the mouth and finger holes, the entire surface is wrapped in cherry bark that has been flattened and cut into a fine tape. The end closer to the mouth hole is called the *kashira* (head) and contains a lead weight that provides balance and increases the sound volume. The end of the head is plugged with a wood block wrapped in gold brocade fabric, and a small carving called a *semi* (cicada) is inset into the underside of the head. The inside of the tube and exterior bark wrapping are usually covered in lacquer.

The ryūteki seen here is wrapped in thin strips of bark and painted with black lacquer on the outside and red lacquer on the inside. The semi is carved in the shape of a dragon. The edges of the mouth hole and finger holes are lined with red lacquer and some edges of the wrapping bark—perhaps where the seams had been coming apart—are mended with red lacquer as well. Although these are later repairs, the distinct contrast of the red against the black lacquer of the bark wrapping creates a vivid accent. This flute is accompanied by its own dedicated case that, in keeping with the name "Ashitazu" (a poetic word for cranes that flock among dense reeds), features maki-e designs of cranes descending toward and standing among the thickly growing reeds along the water. **T.N.**

14.

Hichiriki (flageolet-like instrument) called "Higurashi"

Kamakura period, 13th century
Bamboo wrapped with black lacquered bark strips

Length 7 ¼ inches (18.2 cm)
Tokyo National Museum

The three flutes used in gagaku music, the shō, ryūteki, and hichiriki, are collectively known as the *sankan* (three flutes). The shō represents the sun that shines down from the heavens, the ryūteki represents the voice of the dragon that swims between the heavens and the earth, and the hichiriki represents the voice of the people who inhabit the earth. The hichiriki has a narrower register than both the shō and ryūteki, but it has a loud volume and commands the main melody. The hichiriki was brought to Japan from China, where it is said to have originated in the western regions (Central Asia). It is a small vertical flute made of bamboo with seven finger holes in the front and two on the back. Like the ryūteki, the surface is wrapped in strips of bark, and both the inside of the flute and the bark wrapping are coated in lacquer. It is played by blowing on a reed inserted at the upper end.

The name "Higurashi" refers to a type of cicada that sings "kana kana" in a beautiful high-pitched voice during the twilight hours. As demonstrated by the instruments shown here, names given to musical instruments often relate to animals or insects—such as plovers, cranes, or cicadas—whose songs have elegant associations and perhaps symbolically suggest the pleasing tone of the instrument.

On this hichiriki, black lacquer covers the birch-bark wrapping, and red lacquer lines define the edges of the finger holes. The instrument is accompanied by a fan-shaped storage box made from kassod wood. Chinese characters representing "voice," "scatter," and "ride horseback" appear across the lid of the box, and the characters "tone," "high," "bright," "moon," "beneath," "straw mat," and "before" appear on its sides. These words appear to come from a poem about the flute's namesake cicada, but the complete poem has not yet been identified. **T.N.**

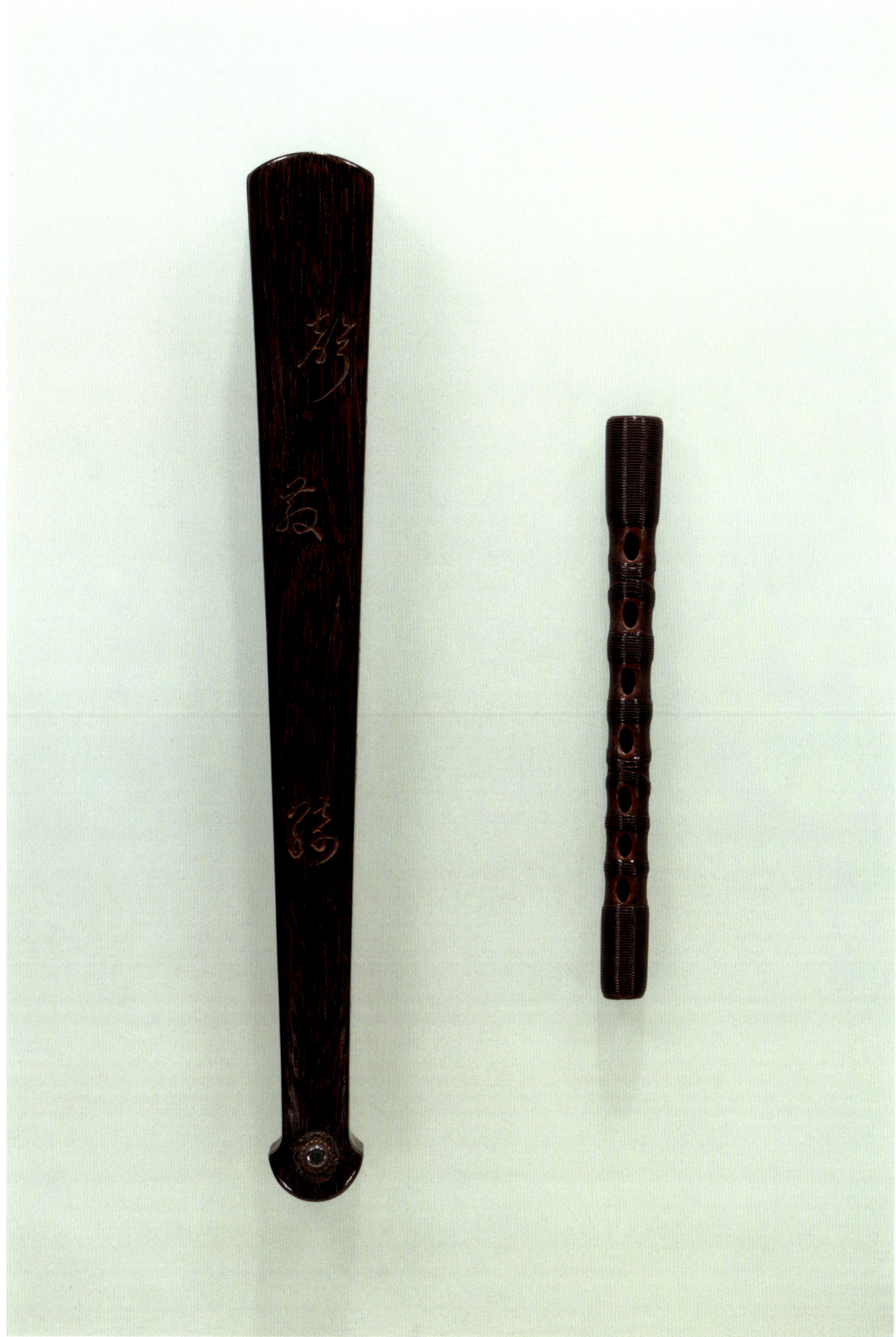

PLATE 14

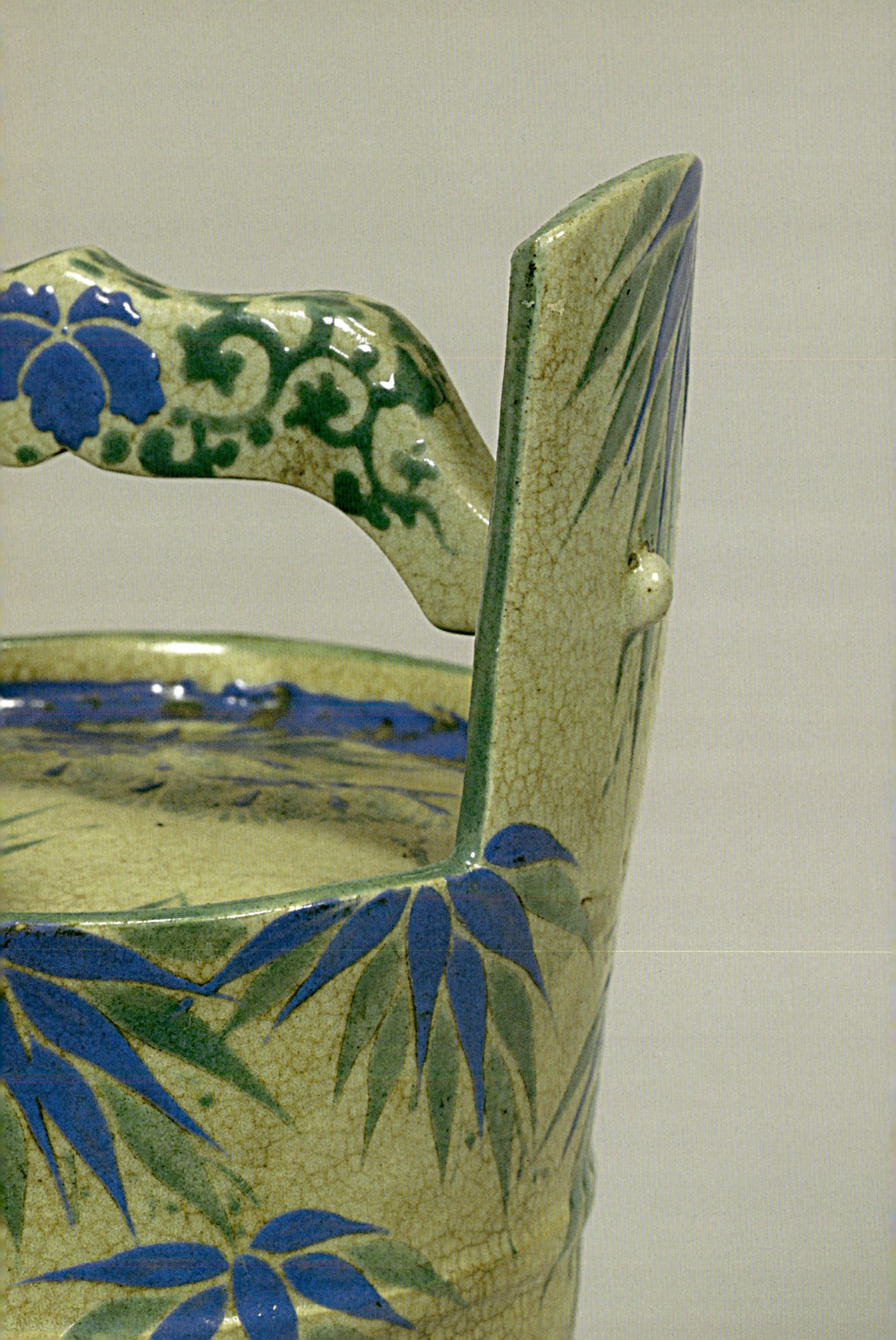

Japanese Ceramics of the Azuchi-Momoyama and Edo Periods

Japanese Ceramics of the Azuchi-Momoyama and Edo Periods

Imai Atsushi

Japanese ceramics evolved under the palpable influence of the ceramic traditions of China and Korea, which not only served as models for technical aspects such as kiln style and glaze chemistry but also shaped features of design, such as vessel form and decorative style. However, with the advent of the *wabi* aesthetic of rustic simplicity advanced by Sen no Rikyū (1522–1591) in the Azuchi-Momoyama period (1573–1603) and the demand it generated for vessels that served specific visual as well as functional roles in the context of the Japanese tea ceremony, Japanese ceramics began to assert a sense of originality through bold deformations and dripping glazes, which distinguished them from their continental models. These new developments included the unglazed wares of regions such as Bizen (in present-day Okayama Prefecture), Shigaraki (in Shiga Prefecture), and Iga (in Mie Prefecture); the uninhibited designs of Shino and Oribe wares produced in the Mino region (present-day Gifu Prefecture); the kilns established in northern Kyushu at Karatsu (present-day Saga and Nagasaki Prefectures) by potters who had emigrated from Korea; and the raku wares that were produced under the direction of tea master Sen no Rikyū to suit his personal tastes. From this period onward, kilns producing works in a wide variety of styles throughout Japan showed an unprecedented degree of creative freedom.

In the 1610s, about the beginning of the Edo period, production of the first porcelain wares in Japan began in Kyushu in Arita, Hizen Province (present-day Saga Prefecture), after Korean potters brought the technique to Japan. These porcelains are collectively known as Imari ware because they were shipped from the port of Imari. Inspired by the underglaze blue-and-white porcelains imported from China that were immensely popular in Japan at the time, Imari wares strove to emulate a Chinese style of design. In the 1640s, the technique of overglaze enamel had made its way to Japan from China, and exports of Imari wares increased when the Dutch East India Company turned to Japan to fill its demand when the supply of porcelains from the Jingdezhen kilns in China was suspended due to political unrest accompanying the transition from the Ming to the Qing dynasty. The beautiful overglaze enamels on a pure white porcelain body known as Kakiemon-style wares, which were perfected at this time, captivated the European aristocracy.

The Nabeshima clan, which controlled Arita, the foremost production center of porcelain wares in Japan, established its own proprietary kiln for producing wares as gifts to the shogunal and daimyo warrior-class families. The shapes and sizes of these products adhered to strict standards, but the refined decorative styles allowed for creative ingenuity, and their designs appear fresh and original even by today's standards. The celebrated Iro-Nabeshima ware, which combined underglaze blue with overglaze enamels, is characterized by a refinement that exercised daring restraint in its limited color palette. Furthermore, the blossoming of an extravagant Genroku culture targeting a newly wealthy merchant class in the late seventeenth century facilitated the rise of a brilliant style of gold-painted porcelain ware known as *kinrande*, a name that likened their elaborate gold designs to the fine patterns woven from gold threads in traditional silk brocade fabrics, called *kinran* in Japanese. By the late Edo period, porcelains had become a deeply ingrained part of people's everyday lives and an even greater variety of motifs were produced, including clever and ingenious designs in underglaze blue.

Also in the Edo period, full-scale ceramic production using high-temperature kilns began in Kyoto, which had proudly stood at the center of Japanese culture since the Heian period (794–1333). The potter Nonomura Seiemon (dates unknown) established the Omuro kiln near the gates of Ninnaji temple in northwest Kyoto about 1647. Taking the "Nin" of Ninnaji and the "Sei" of Seiemon, he went by the name Ninsei. Under the patronage of the tea master Kanamori Sōwa (1584–1657), Ninsei started to make tea wares and opened up a new path for himself with his magnificent ceramic painting style that made brilliant use of red, gold, and silver pigments. Ogata Kenzan (1663–1743), the third son of a kimono merchant in Kyoto and the younger brother of the eminent painter Ogata Kōrin (1658–1716), studied pottery at Ninsei's Omuro kiln and created tableware rich with literary allusion, breathing a new spirit into ceramics through collaborations with his brother Kōrin. In the late Edo period, Okuda Eisen (1753–1811) succeeded in producing hard-paste porcelain wares for the first time in Kyoto. He later cultivated many students who became master craftsmen, including Aoki Mokubei (1767–1833), Kinkodō Kisuke (1765–1837), and Ninnami Dōhachi (1783–1855). They assiduously studied both domestic and foreign ancient ceramics and produced sophisticated ceramic wares that were modeled on earlier examples while also incorporating their own original innovations.

In the late Edo period, new kilns producing Banko ware (in present-day Mie Prefecture), Tobe ware (in present-day Ehime Prefecture), Mushiake ware (in present-day Okayama Prefecture), and many others prospered throughout Japan, vying for individuality by producing ceramics that reflected the traditions and features of their respective regions. As a result, the ceramic arts in Japan have been passed down to the present as a traditional manufacturing industry rooted in specific regions across Japan.

15.

Square Dish with Autumn Grasses Design

Nezumi-Shino type, Mino ware
Azuchi-Momoyama to Edo period, 16th–17th century
Glazed stoneware

7 ½ x 9 ⅞ inches (19 x 22.5 cm), height 1 ¾ inches (4.5 cm)
Tokyo National Museum

Shino wares were a new type of white ceramic produced in the Mino region (present-day southeastern Gifu Prefecture) from the Azuchi-Momoyama period to the early Edo period. They utilized a feldspar glaze, which turned a milky white color when fired at a high temperature of more than 1,200 degrees Celsius. Variations of Shino ware include Muji-Shino (plain Shino), in simple white, E-Shino (picture Shino), with painted designs in iron pigment on a white ground, and Nezumi-Shino (mouse-gray Shino), which is the reverse of the E-Shino technique.

In Nezumi-Shino wares, the white clay body is covered completely with a slip of iron-rich red clay known as *oni-ita*, which is then covered with feldspar glaze. Designs are made by scratching away parts of the oni-ita layer to reveal the white surface underneath. After the glaze has been applied and the piece has been fired, the white designs appear on a gray ground. Another technique involves painting designs in iron pigment inside the random spaces that happen to remain unglazed when applying the red clay.

The plate seen here is known as a "frame plate" (*gaku-zara*) because the pattern around the edge of the dish resembles a frame. This style is a specialty of Nezumi-Shino. The rectangular dish has shallow grooves at each of the four corners, and the tips of the corners have been rounded. Four round feet are attached to the bottom. The design on the face of the dish features a rock at the center surrounded by wind-blown grasses. This motif of autumnal plants appears frequently in Japanese decorative-art objects. **Y.A.**

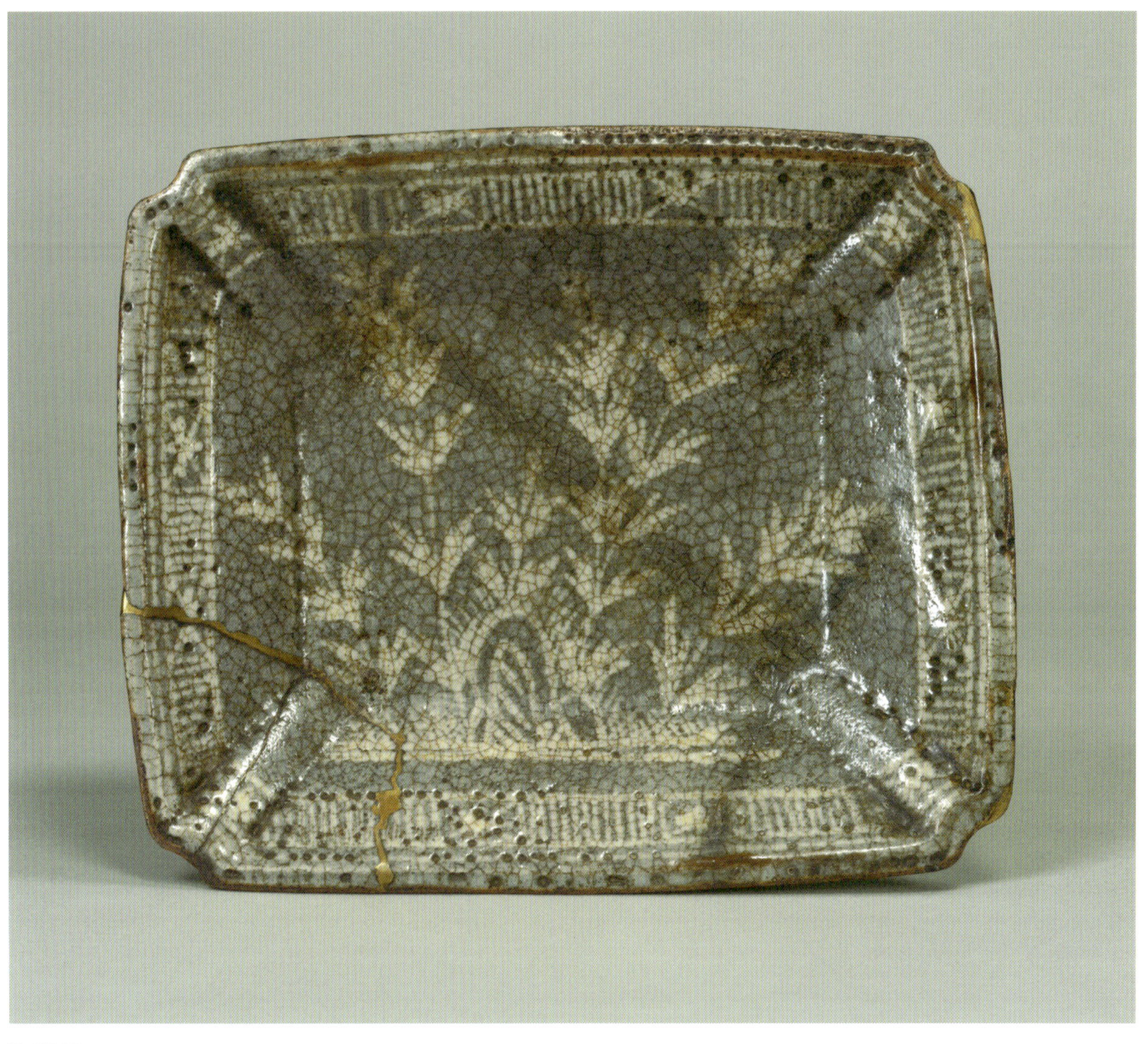

PLATE 15

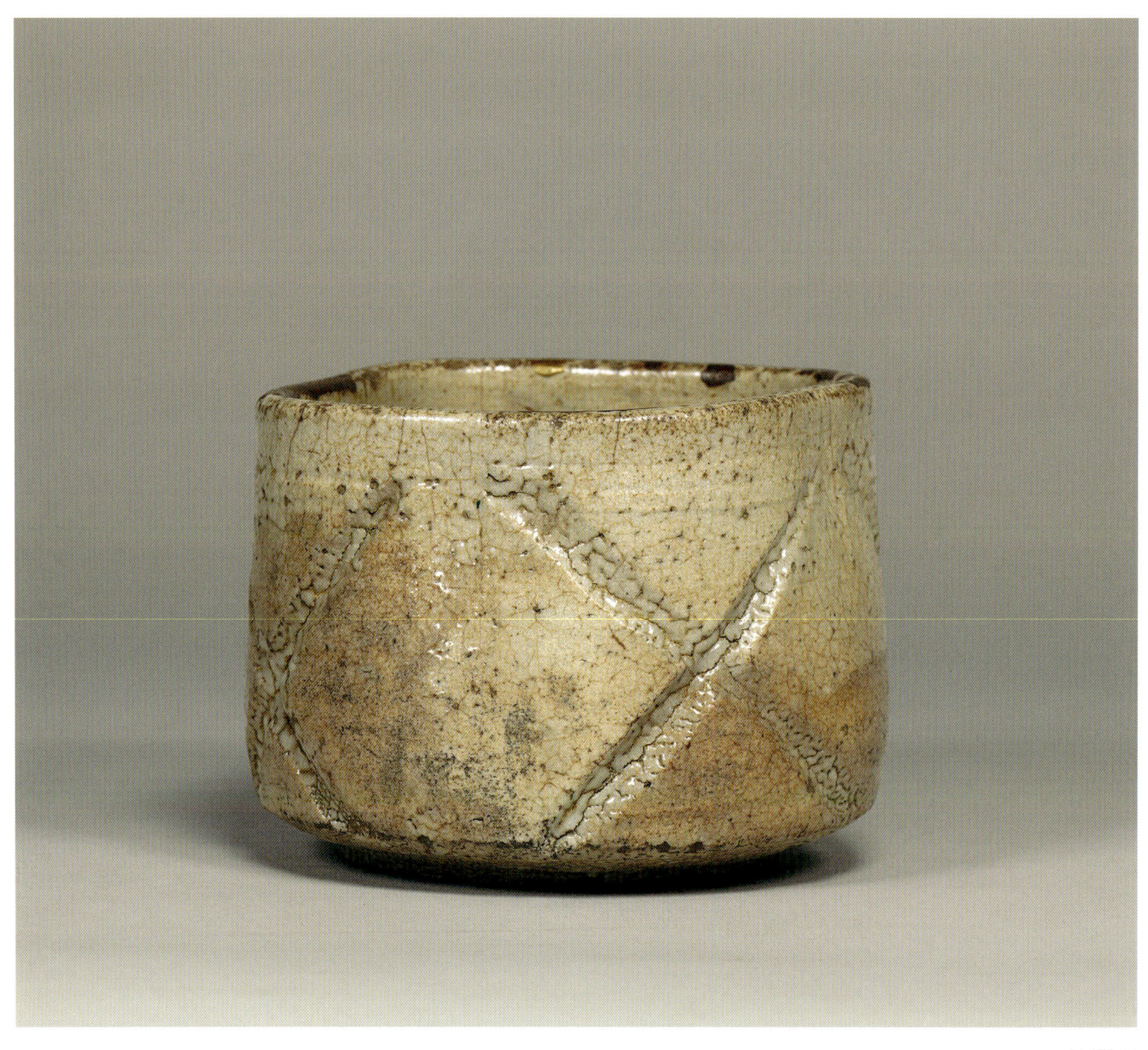

PLATE 16

16.

Tea Bowl

Hori (carved) Karatsu type, Karatsu ware
Azuchi-Momoyama to Edo period, 16th–17th century
Glazed stoneware

Height 3 7/8 inches (9.9 cm); diameter of mouth 4 1/2–4 3/4 inches (11.5–12 cm);
diameter of bottom 3 3/8 inches (8.7 cm)
Gift of Mr. Hirota Matsushige
Tokyo National Museum

Karatsu ware was produced in western Saga and northern Nagasaki prefectures and was named for the port of Karatsu in Saga prefecture, from which it was distributed. It purportedly originated with Korean potters who came to Japan following Toyotomi Hideyoshi's (1536–1598) two military acts against Korea, known as the Bunroku and Keichō campaigns. Karatsu ware enjoys a wide stylistic range, including works with Korean influences and those that share similar attributes to Mino ware. Many great tea bowls were produced in this region, giving rise to its great acclaim among tea masters, who ranked its tea bowls particularly highly, often as one of the three best wares in all of Japan.

This carved Karatsu tea bowl bears designs carved into the clay body of the bowl, over which a feldspar glaze is applied. The body of the tea bowl is pressed on all sides, forming a quadrangular tube shape when viewed from above. Relative to the short foot, the body is deep and somewhat large for a tea bowl, offering a solid sense of substance when held in the hands. The fissured texturing of the glaze, known as *kairagi* (sharkskin), which appears on the foot ring and especially along the X-shaped hatch marks carved into each side of the bowl, gives it an intensity that contributes to the majestic aura of this tea bowl. **Y.A.**

17.

Water Jar with Handles

Iga ware
Edo period, 17th century
Natural ash-glazed stoneware

Height 7 ¾ inches (19.5 cm); diameter of mouth 5 ⅞ inches (14.9 cm)
Tokyo National Museum

Iga ware was made in present-day northwestern Mie Prefecture from the Azuchi-Momoyama period to the Edo period. Along with the spread of the rustic aesthetic in the tea ceremony (*wabicha*) from the end of the Muromachi period, demand grew among tea masters for rough, simple tea wares, and they actively began to commission such wares from kilns in various regions. As a result of this trend, Iga soon became prized as a model kiln. Iga ware included thick-walled and highly modulated shapes freely patterned with scraped or beaten marks on the surface; it also featured the signature natural glaze process created by ash in the kiln melting against the unglazed vessel when fired under high temperature. Thus, though these Iga wares were seemingly naive in their simplicity, they were produced with a conscious ingenuity of design that resulted in many highly individualized works.

This Iga water jar has handles on both sides and visible marks from the turning of the potter's wheel across the neck and body intersected by spatula marks and pronounced vertical cracks from the firing process, leaving a dynamic impression. A green vitreous glaze coats a portion of the mouth and runs from the shoulder down to the bottom of the jar, which is indented in three sections to form the feet, giving the piece a look of solidity.

In the tea ceremony, water jars serve as vessels for fresh water for replenishing the kettle and cleansing the tea bowls. Placed in the customary position of prominence next to the kettle in front of the host, this water jar would certainly be a particularly strong presence at a tea gathering. **Y.A.**

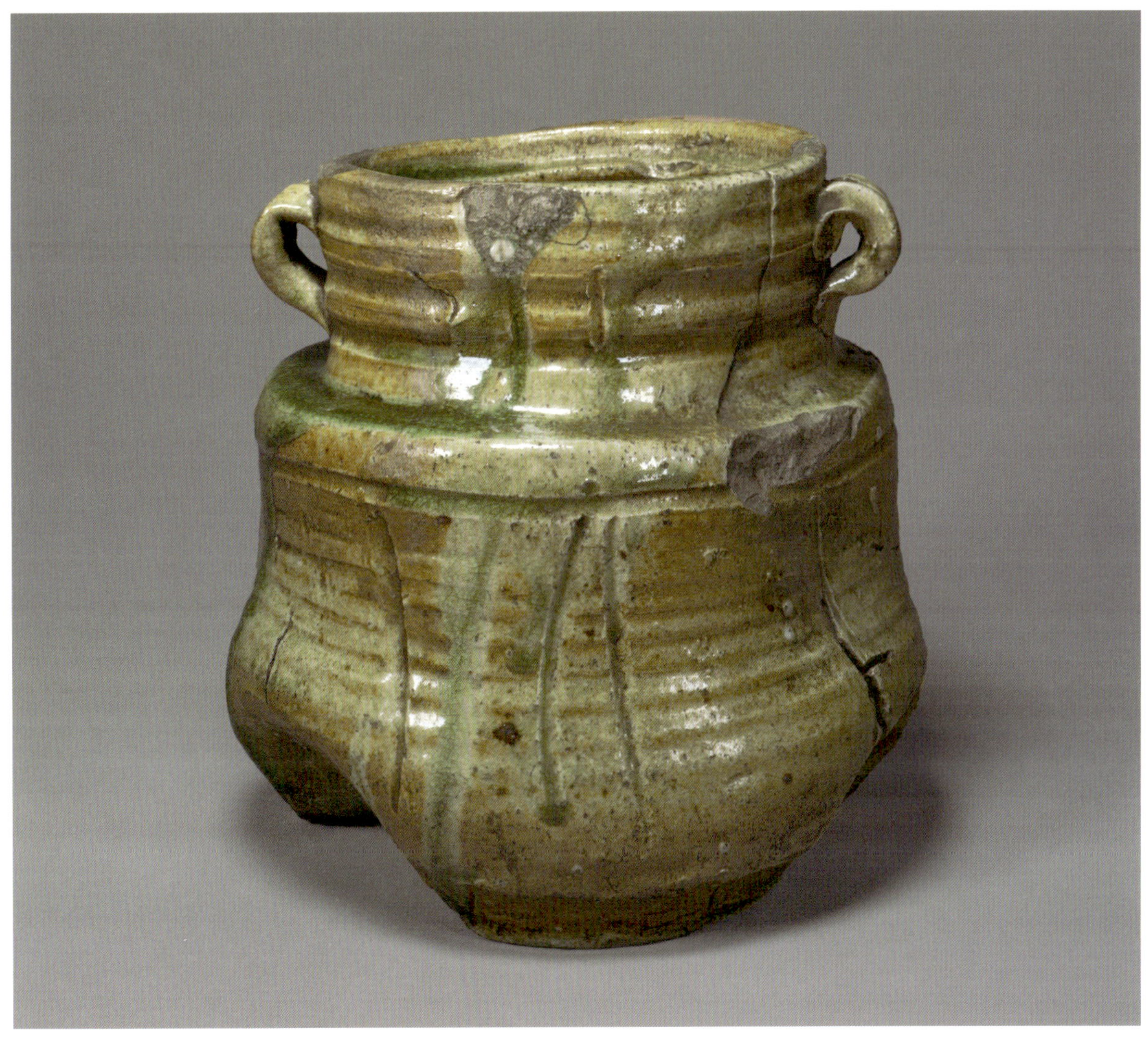

PLATE 17

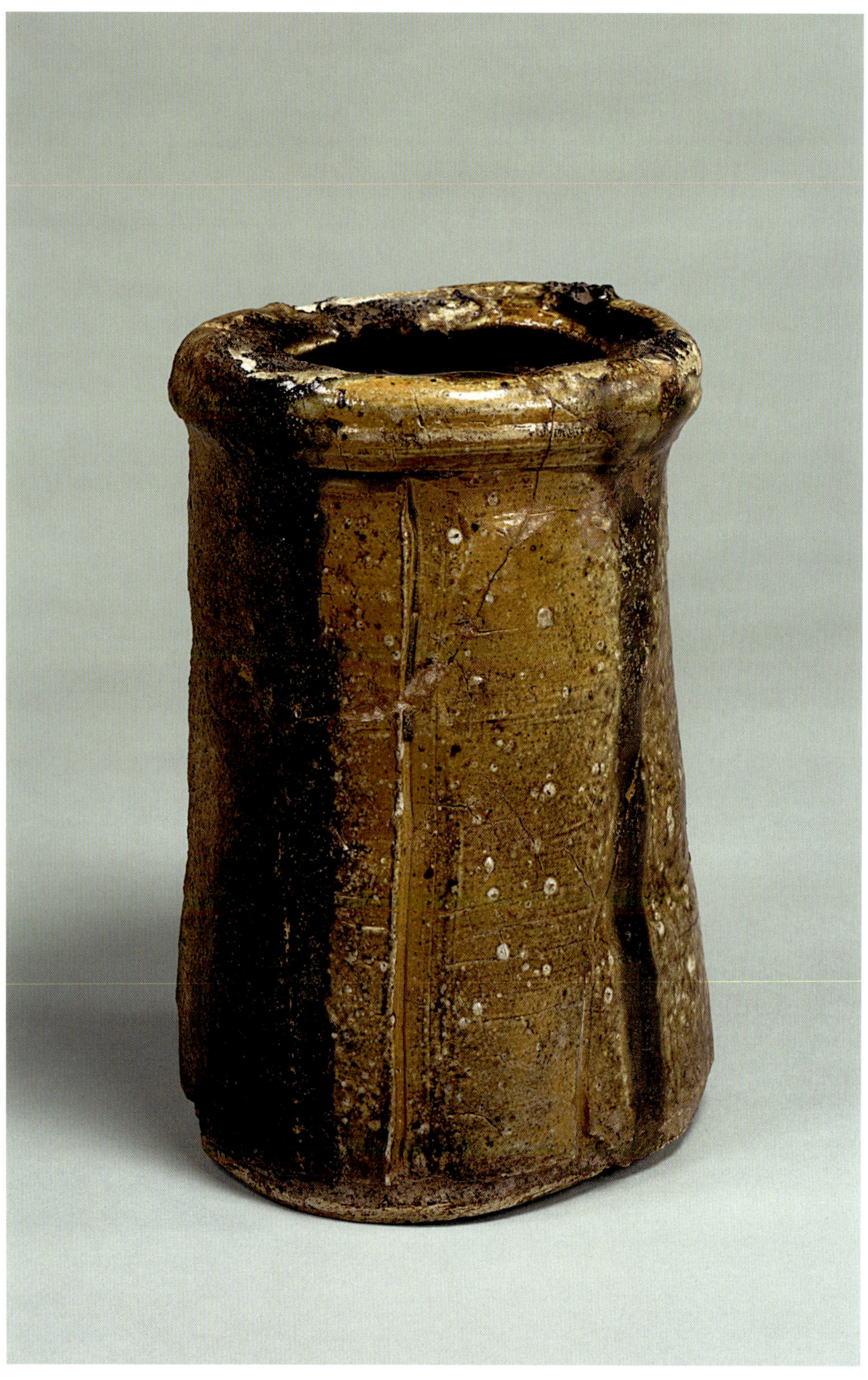

PLATE 18

18.

Flower Vase with Square Mouth

Iga ware
Edo period, 17th century
Natural ash-glazed stoneware

Height 6 ⅝ inches (16.8 cm); diameter of mouth 4 ¾ inches (12.3 cm);
diameter of bottom 4 ¼ inches (11 cm)
Tokyo National Museum

In addition to water jars, Iga ware was renowned for its many exceptional flower vases. In the tea ceremony, flowers serve to create the mood of the season. Naturally, much importance has been attached to the vessels that hold them. In the Muromachi period, bronzes, celadon porcelains, and other imported Chinese wares were the most prized for this purpose, but as rustic tastes in tea ceremony prospered, bamboo flower vases and domestically produced ceramics were sought after as being more suited to these simple tastes.

This cylindrical Iga flower vase widens slightly toward the bottom, reminiscent of a traditional portable travel pillow, for which this type of shape is named. The body is fired under high temperature with three stripes of black ash glaze running down from the edge of the thick mouth to the bottom. One side of the body exhibits a reddish tinge with distinct spatula markings, while the clay surface reveals many of the small embedded bits of feldspar that are distinctive of Iga ware. The other side of the body offers a completely different perspective with its burnt-black surface and ash glaze. A ring attached to the upper portion of the black side suggests that this flower vase was intended to be hung on the alcove pillar in a tea room. **Y.A.**

19.

Pail-shaped Sake Cask with Design of Pine and Bamboo

Kyoto ware
Edo period, 18th century
Glazed stoneware with overglaze enamels

Height 7 ¾ inches (19.6 cm);
diameter 5 inches (12.6 cm);
diameter of bottom 3 ⅛ inches (7.8 cm)
Tokyo National Museum

This *sake* vessel imitates the shape of a wooden keg, or *tsunodaru*, that is used for sending congratulatory gifts of sake. The two raised bands around the body of the vessel represent the hoops of the wooden barrel. A pale brown glaze covers the entire surface, except for the bottom, and is overlaid with a design of pine and bamboo painted in blue and green overglaze enamels. Pine and bamboo are both popular auspicious motifs because neither loses its green color even in the midst of the harsh cold of winter. Rendered in thickly painted pigments, the branch motif extends up the sides of the vessel and continues across the top, while curling arabesques adorn both sides of the crosspiece of the handle. In addition, the left side of the underside bears a potter's mark, but it is illegible.

Full-scale ceramic production in Kyoto is believed to have begun at about the end of the sixteenth or the beginning of the seventeenth century. Here, in the city that had represented the center of Japanese culture since the Heian period, potters went beyond the simply practical to produce elegant ceramics in a rich variety of different shapes. A refined and subdued color palette, consisting primarily of blues and greens, is also typical of Kyoto ware. **I.A.**

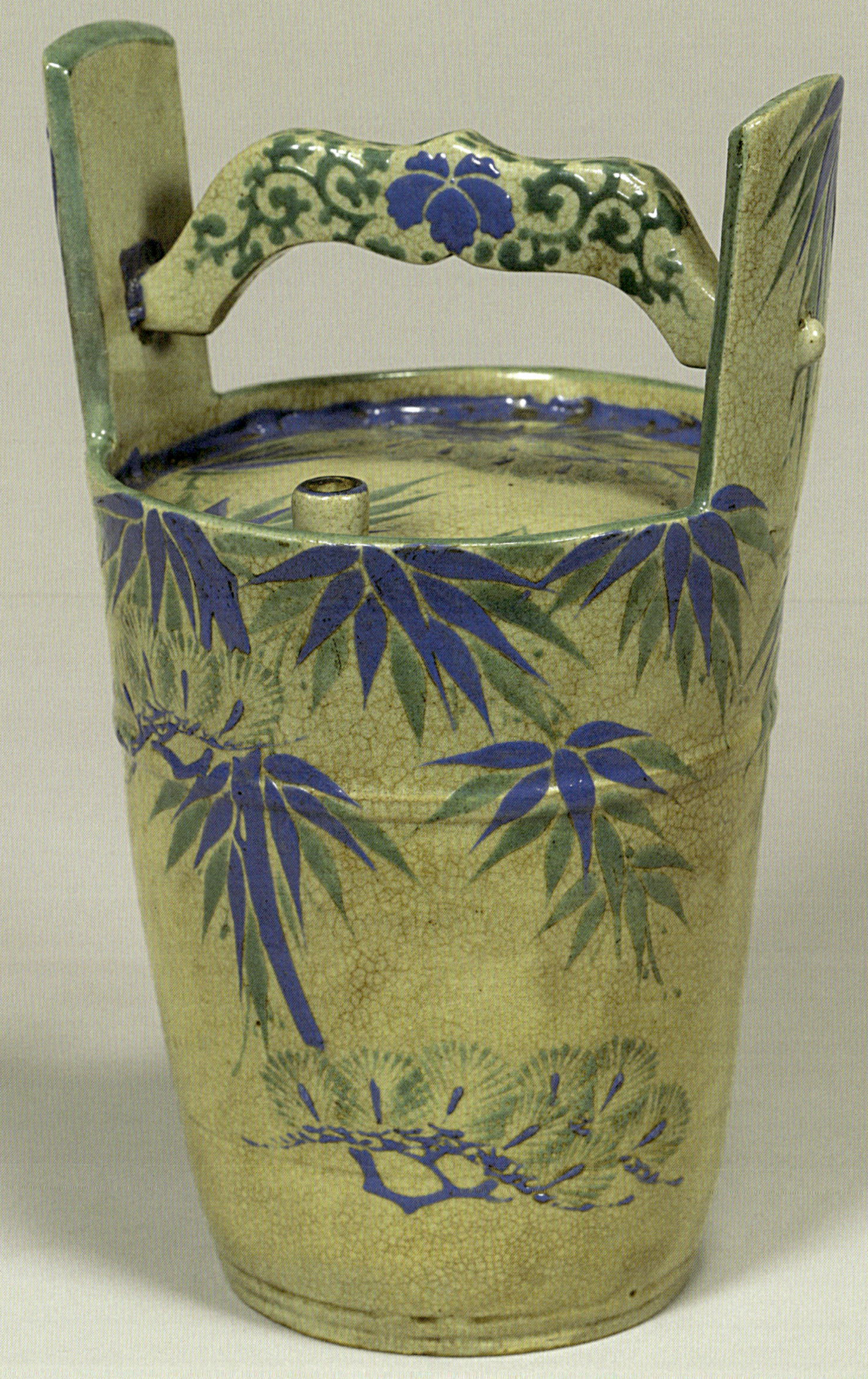

PLATE 19

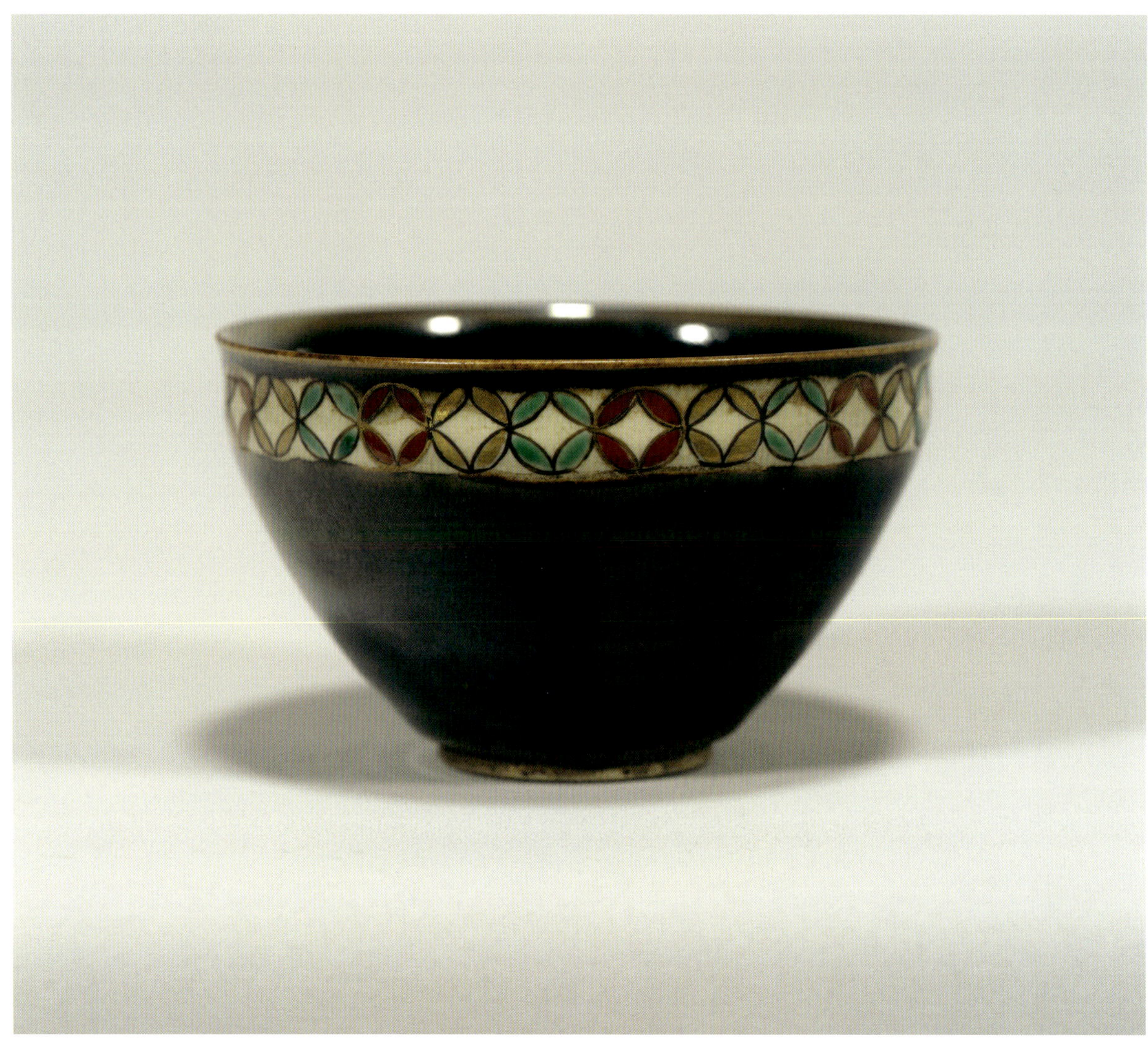

PLATE 20

20.

Tenmoku Tea Bowl with Interlocking Circle Design

Kyoto ware, with mark "Iwakurayama"
Edo period, 18th century
Glazed stoneware with overglaze enamels

Height 2 ½ inches (6.3 cm);
diameter of mouth 4 ¼ inches (10.9 cm);
diameter of bottom 1 ⅝ inches (4.1 cm)
Tokyo National Museum

This vessel shape, recessed slightly below the rim and then narrowing gently toward the foot, emulates the Tianmu (*tenmoku* in Japanese) wares that were made in China's Fujian Province and brought to Japan in great numbers during the Kamakura period (1192–1333). In the Muromachi period, Chinese *yōhen* tenmoku from the Jin-dynasty kilns were esteemed most highly, followed by *yuteki* tenmoku. As the rustic *wabi* style of tea ceremony became popular, *haikatsugi* tenmoku, with its low-luster and richly varied glazes, also came to be appreciated. Considered the standard bowls for drinking tea, haikatsugi tenmoku wares were enthusiastically copied in Japan in the area of Seto (present-day Aichi Prefecture) as well.

This tenmoku bowl was created in Kyoto in the Edo period. The shape of the base follows that of haikatsugi tenmoku, with a distinct edge formed during the carving of the foot ring. However, the addition of a striking overglaze enamel decoration not seen in Chinese tenmoku bowls reveals the Japanese taste of the time. The surface was covered in a black glaze, except for a band in a clear glaze just below the rim. A pattern of linked circles was then applied in red, green, and gold enamels, after which the bowl was fired again in a small specialty kiln for firing overglaze enamel, known as a *kingama*. In the linked-circle pattern, the greens and golds are outlined in black, and the reds are outlined in gold. The side of the foot ring bears a seal reading "Iwakurayama." **I.A.**

21.

Dish with Design of Dandelions

Nabeshima ware
Edo period, 18th century
Glazed porcelain with overglaze enamels

Height 2 ⅛ inches (5.4 cm);
diameter 8 inches (20.2 cm);
diameter of foot 4 ¼ inches (10.8 cm)
Tokyo National Museum

Porcelain production in Japan began in Arita (present-day Saga Prefecture), northern Kyushu, at the beginning of the Edo period. The Nabeshima clan, which claimed Arita within its domain, established an officially administered kiln to produce wares for gifts to the shogunal and daimyo families. The finest techniques were unreservedly applied to these wares, and the designs were exceedingly refined. Most Nabeshima wares are relatively deep dishes with a high foot, and their shape and size strictly follow an official standard.

Works that concurrently utilize underglaze blue in combination with overglaze enamel pigments are called Iro-Nabeshima ware. Designs for this dish, prepared in advance as sketches, were transferred onto the surface of the porcelain body in steady brushwork. The dandelion, a familiar spring flower, is chosen as the subject, and the blossoms, normally yellow, are daringly rendered in red. Three-dimensionality and the overlapping of the flowers are suggested by the very small, unpainted area just inside the outlines of the slender petals. As a general rule, the color palette of Iro-Nabeshima wares was limited to underglaze blue (indigo) and overglaze red, green, and yellow, demonstrating an avoidance of excess that is distinctively characteristic of Nabeshima wares. In accordance with the general rules of Nabeshima ware during the height of their production, an underglaze linked-circle design covers three sides of the outer surface of the dish and a comb-tooth pattern adorns the foot. **I.A.**

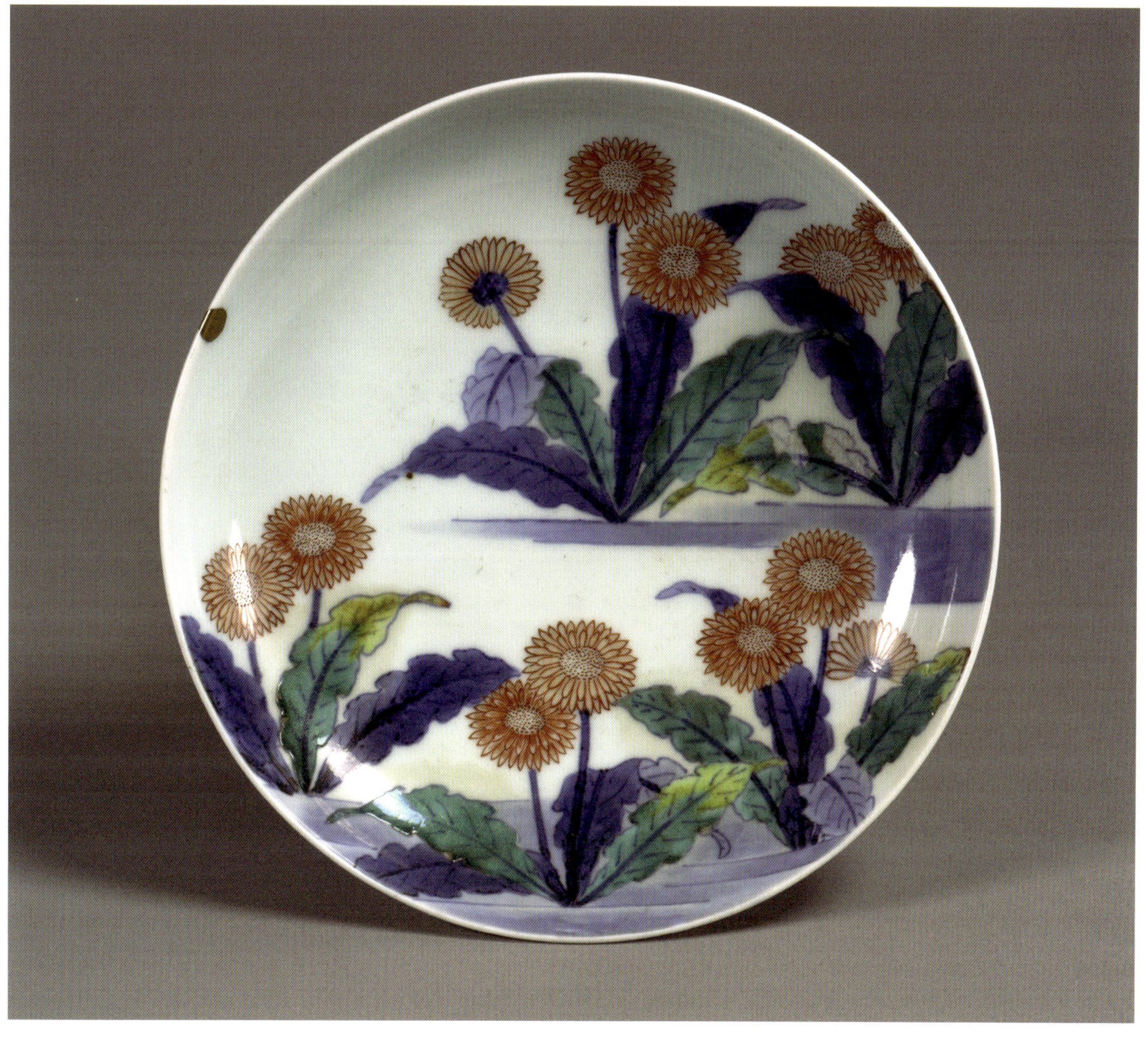

PLATE 21

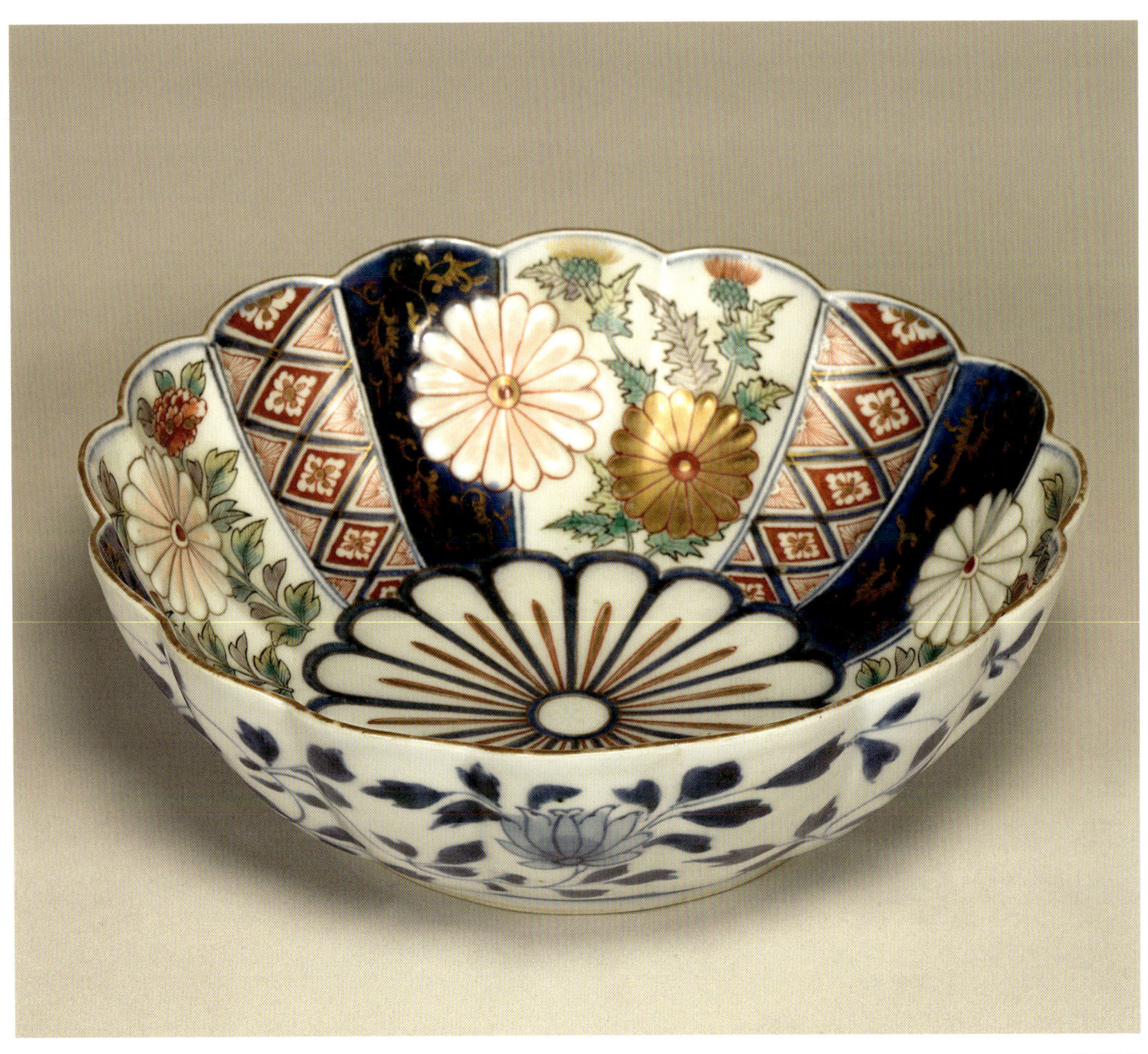

PLATE 22

22.
Chrysanthemum-shaped Bowl with Design of Chrysanthemums

Imari ware
Edo period, 18th century
Glazed porcelain with overglaze enamels

Height 3 inches (7.5 cm);
diameter of mouth 9 inches (22.8 cm);
diameter of foot 5 inches (12.8 cm)
Tokyo National Museum

Starting at about the end of the seventeenth century, splendid porcelains adorned with lavish gold glazes began to be produced for members of Japan's wealthy merchant class. These were known as *kinrande* ware because their elaborate designs were reminiscent of brocade fabrics (*kinran*) whose fine patterns were woven from gold thread. While emulating the model of gold-painted porcelains of China's late-Ming-dynasty (1368–1644) Jingdezhen kilns, the shapes and designs of these vessels also reflect the incorporation of Japanese taste.

This bowl is mold-formed into the shape of a chrysanthemum flower with sixteen petals. An additional chrysanthemum design is impressed at the center, and, conversely, chrysanthemum flowers positioned at the four corners of the outer edge are rendered in relief. A generous application of many colors—red, green, purple, yellow, black, and gold over an underglaze indigo ground—depicts chrysanthemums, thistles, peonies, linked diamonds, and floral arabesques, demonstrating the fashion of an era that valued pomp and splendor. On the outer surface, Buddhist *hōsōge* flower arabesques are rendered in underglaze blue. **I.A.**

23.

Four-lobed Bowl with Design of Cherry Blossoms and Maple Trees

By Takahashi Dōhachi II (Ninnami Dōhachi, 1783–1855), with mark "Dōhachi"
Edo period, 19th century
Glazed stoneware with overglaze enamels

Height 3 ½ inches (8.8 cm);
diameter of mouth 6 ½ inches (16.5 cm);
diameter of bottom 3 ⅛ inches (7.9 cm)
Tokyo National Museum

The potter Takahashi Dōhachi II (1783–1855) was active in Kyoto in the latter part of the Edo period. He went by the name "Ninnami," which was a combination of the characters "Nin" and "Ami," honorary names that he was granted from Ninnaji temple and Daigoji Sanbōin temple respectively. He attained a high level of technical skill through assiduous research of both domestic and foreign ancient ceramics, and specialized in copying Korean tea bowls and Kyoto wares. He was particularly captivated by the work of ceramic artist Ogata Kenzan (1663–1743), the great pioneer of Kyoto ware who had forged a new path in the field of tableware through his rich use of literary associations. Dōhachi produced many masterpieces that reinterpreted Kenzan's style through his own adaptations.

This bowl by Dōhachi achieves variation in the form through indentations in the four sides of its elliptical shape. Underglaze iron and white clay pigments combined with overglaze reds and greens portray the spring cherry tree with its pale pink blossoms and the red-leafed maple of autumn. This pairing of motifs is known as *unkinde* (cloud-brocade style), where the cherry blossoms represent clouds and the maple leaves represent brocade. Inspired by Ogata Kōrin's *Large Bowl with Cherry Blossoms* and *Large Bowl with Maple Leaves*, Dōhachi devised this pairing, which enjoyed great favor for allowing the appreciation of the seasonality of spring and autumn at the same time. A framed inscription "Kenzan" next to the trunk of the maple tree on the outside of the bowl pays homage to Ogata Kenzan. A seal reading "Dōhachi" is stamped inside the foot on the left side. I.A.

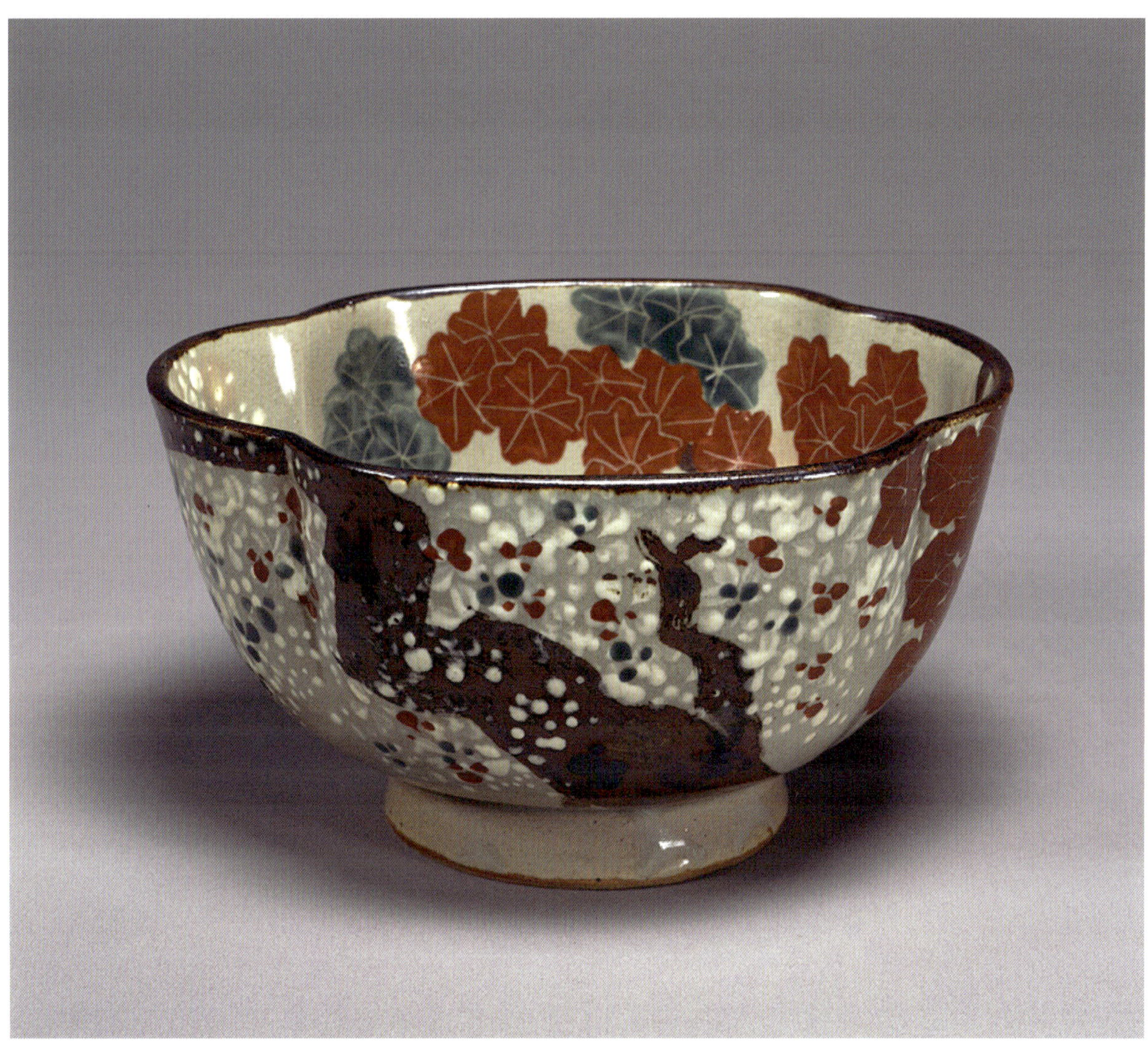

PLATE 23

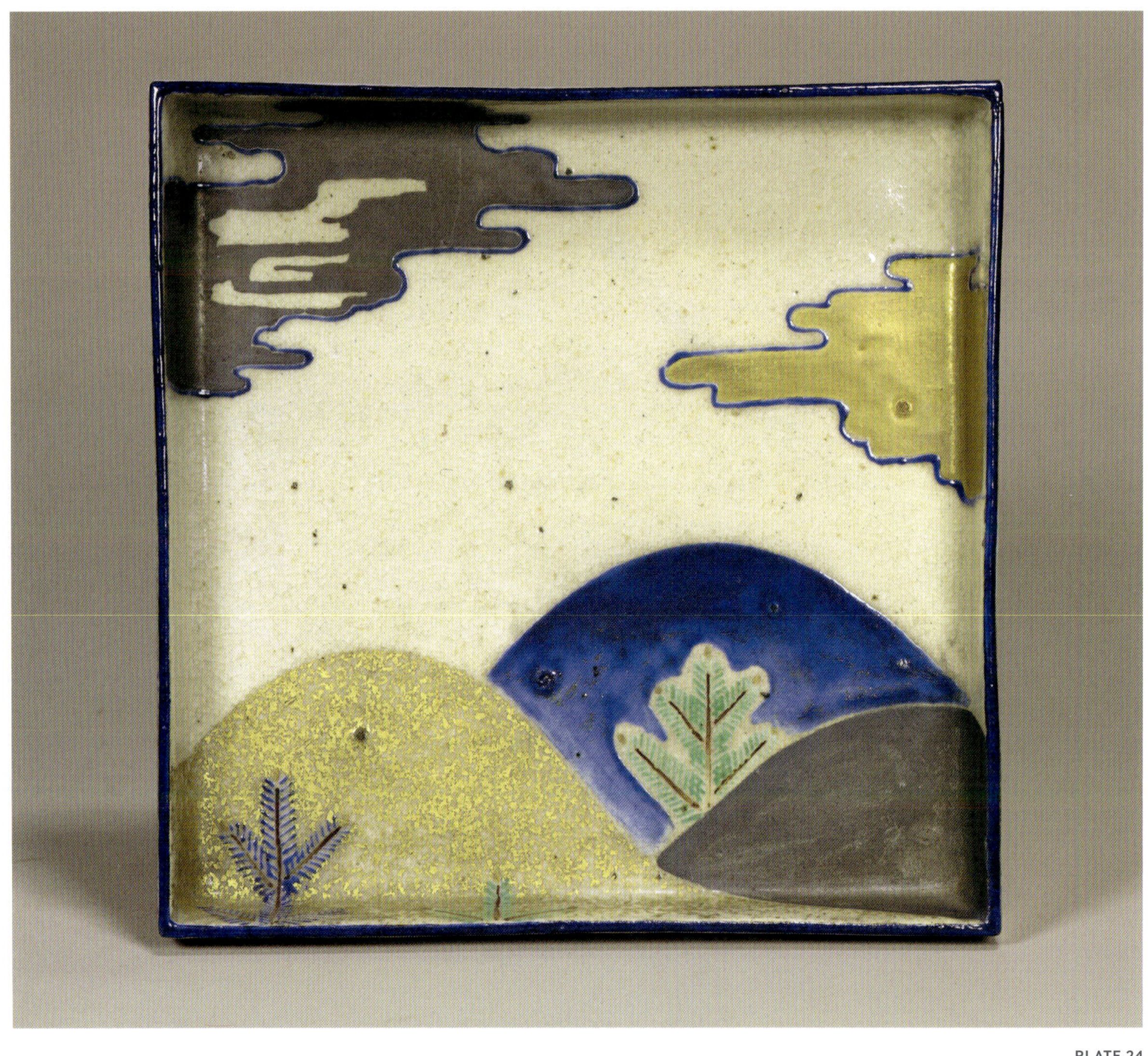

PLATE 24

24.

Square Dish with Design of Young Pines and Distant Mountains

By Eiraku Wazen (1823–1896)
Edo–Meiji period, 19th century
Glazed porcelain with overglaze enamels

1 ½ x 8 ½ x 8 ¼ inches (3.7 x 21.5 x 20.9 cm)
Tokyo National Museum

The potter Eiraku Wazen was active in Kyoto from the late Edo period to the Meiji period. He was born the eldest son of potter Eiraku Hozen and in 1843 succeeded to the name Eiraku Zengorō XII, a hereditary title that he held until taking the name Wazen upon retirement. He not only was skillful in copying great Chinese tea-ware styles such as overglaze Swatow ware, so-called old blue-and-white ware (*kosometsuke* in Japanese), Shonzui ware, and others, but also admired Japanese artists, such as Nonomura Ninsei and Ogata Kenzan, of the Kyoto ceramic tradition, and formulated a modern style infused with new and original ideas.

This square plate with low-rising vertical sides is modeled upon the square dishes that were Kenzan's specialty. On the inside surface of the plate, an image of clouds and mountains interspersed with young pine trees is painted in overglaze blue, green, brown, gold, and silver. The young pine, which grows vigorously and retains its green color even through the winter's bitter cold, is an auspicious design symbolizing spring and the New Year. The generous use of silver offers a novel sense of color. A pattern of interlinked circles painted in blue and gold overglaze pigments lines the outside edges of the vertical sides, and the unglazed bottom bears a seal reading "Eiraku" at the center. I.A.

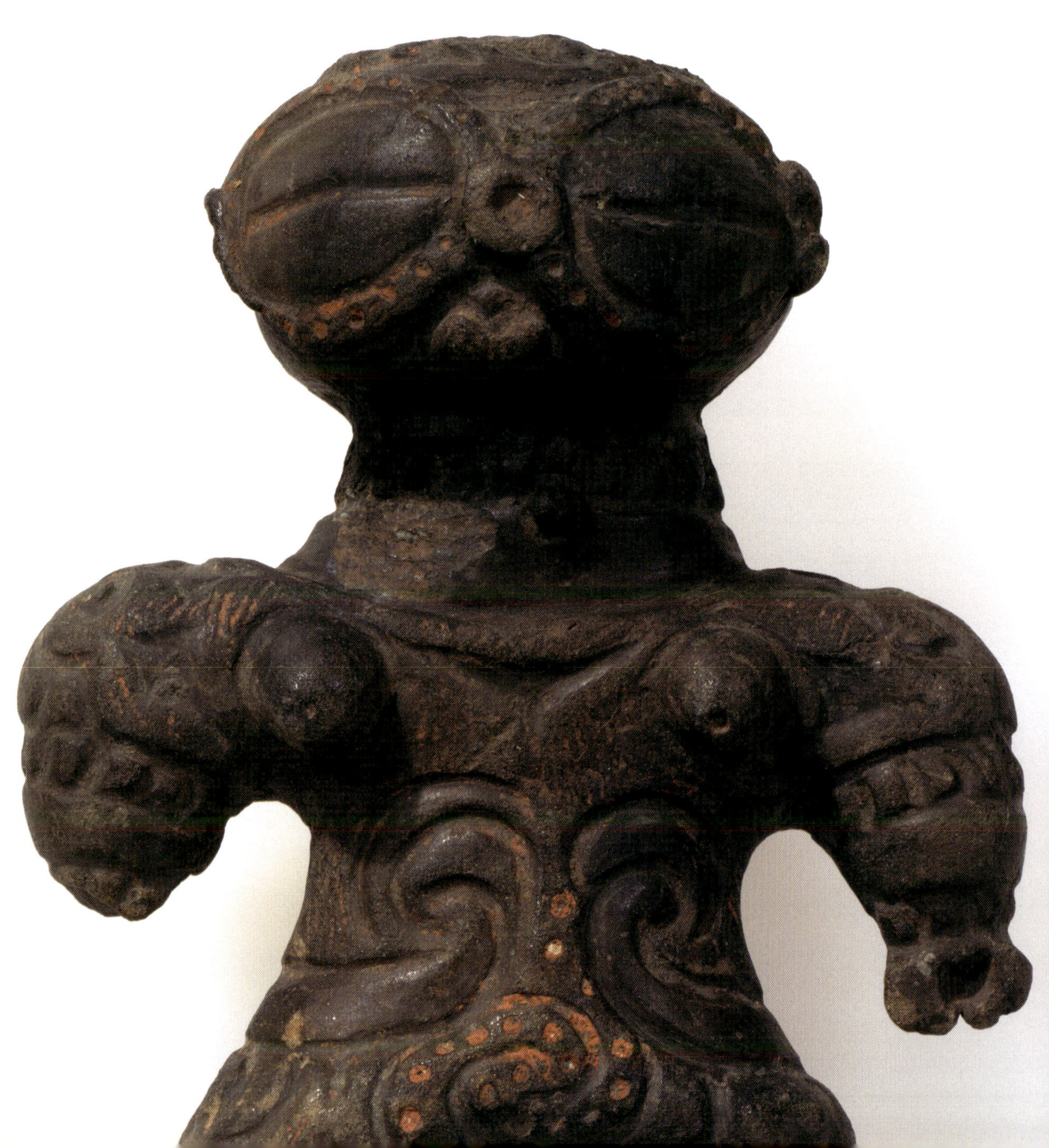

Jōmon-period Pottery and Clay Figurines

Jōmon-period Pottery and Clay Figurines

Shinagawa Yoshiya

It is believed that humans first started inhabiting the Japanese archipelago approximately thirty thousand years ago. The period spanning from the end of the Ice Age (c. 10,000 B.C.) to 400 B.C. was an extended Neolithic era called the Jōmon period, during which people obtained their food not through agriculture or raising livestock but rather through hunting, fishing, and gathering. Typically, the invention of earthenware pottery and the use of bows and arrows in combination with a move toward the formation of permanent settlements are recognized as the indicators of the start of the Jōmon period, whereas the beginning of rice farming and the use of metal tools are seen as indicators of its end. By the Jōmon period, rising temperatures had resulted in the extinction of large animals such as the Naumann elephant and giant Irish elk. The smaller, nimbler animals, such as boars and deer, that replaced them became targets of human hunting. The archaeological discovery of mounds of discarded seashells and other waste further suggests that larger fishing grounds were created as sea levels rose to form bays and inlets. Moreover, the invention of pottery made a number of advances possible, such as the ability to cook food, making it easier to digest, the availability of effective sterilization, which resulted in better health, and cooking and storage capabilities, which expanded the diet to include a greater variety of vegetables. It is believed that this new capacity to obtain a great variety of foodstuffs efficiently and reliably, cook them, and preserve and store them allowed Jōmon society to develop a more sedentary lifestyle.

A variety of tools were made and used throughout the Jōmon era. They can be divided into two major groups: functional, known as primary tools, and nonfunctional, or secondary tools. Functional tools include objects that were used for acquiring food, such as hooks and stone weights for fishing, or arrowheads and spears for hunting. They also include food-preparation tools, such as earthenware containers for storage or for cooking, grinding stones for crushing nuts, and stone plates, as well as manufacturing tools, such as axes and drills. In contrast, the purpose of the nonfunctional implements is not easily identifiable from their shape, and they are generally believed to have served some ceremonial purpose.

The primary tools were made from a variety of raw materials, including stone, wood, animal bone and horn, and shell. Of these tools, unglazed Jōmon earthenware, formed from clay and heat-fired, were produced in the greatest numbers and are the most representative artifacts of the period. Jōmon wares varied widely in both modeling and style depending on the time periods and geographic regions in which they were produced, but careful analysis of the shapes and designs reveals certain chronological transitions in style and illuminates certain regional differences. Historically, the development of Jōmon pottery can be divided roughly into six periods: the Incipient Jōmon period (c. 10,000–7,000 B.C.), the Initial Jōmon period (7,000–4,000 B.C.), Early Jōmon period (4,000–3,000 B.C.), Middle Jōmon period (3,000–2,000 B.C.), Late Jōmon period (2,000–1,000 B.C.), and Final Jōmon period (1,000–400 B.C.).

Jōmon wares were not formed on a wheel but rather were typically coil-built, or else molded by hand in the case of small pieces. It is postulated that they were fired in open pits, most likely at a low temperature of about six hundred degrees Celsius (eleven hundred degrees Fahrenheit). Created by rolling twisted rope across the raw clay surface of these earthenware vessels, the decorating technique from which the name of the period was drawn (*jō mon* means "cord-marked") was used consistently from the Incipient Jōmon period through the Final Jōmon period. Many other types of designs were also applied by pressing bamboo, shells, or other tools against the surface or by affixing ropes of clay to the surface of the pots. In the Middle Jōmon period, three-dimensional decorative techniques developed, among which were the "flame-shaped" jars, so named for their elaborately carved decorative rims that flared upward like rising flames. The first Jōmon earthenwares were deep jars for cooking, and, as time progressed, additional types of vessels emerged, such as shallower pots and bowls for serving or storing food, followed by jars, then vessels for pouring liquids. This development is attributed to an increased sophistication in food preparation and the further distinction between vessels used for serving and those used for storage. Not only were earthenware vessels used as containers for transporting foodstuffs, but they soon became objects of exchange themselves, and in a few cases were even used as burial caskets, suggesting that they served a widespread and diverse role in Jōmon society.

The secondary implements were also made from a wide variety of materials, but the most representative pieces in this category are figurines, masks, and animal-shaped objects made from clay, and poles, swords, and figurines made from stone. To date, more than eighteen thousand unglazed clay figurines in the shape of human figures have been discovered and are celebrated not only for what they reveal about the spiritual belief system of the Jōmon period but also for the insights they provide into the everyday customs of the Jōmon people, such as their hairstyles and tattoos.

In the Incipient Jōmon period, simplified carvings of the upper human torso were produced in the Kinki region, and by the Early Jōmon period, heads, arms, and legs were added to represent full-body figures on flat slabs. In the Middle Jōmon period, these figures became three-dimensional statues that could stand on their own, and from the Late Jōmon to the Final Jōmon period, the popularity of these figurines, known as *dogū*, spread to northern and eastern Japan.

From their very earliest form, these clay figurines had breasts, indicating that the primary purpose of dogū was to represent the female gender. Later, many examples appeared with the addition of swollen bellies with bands across the center, which are thought to represent pregnancy. Consequently, it is believed that these figurines were used in rituals of childbirth, fertility, or rebirth. Many figurines have been discovered only in fragmentary form, and they may have been destroyed as substitutes for human illness or injury. On the other hand, some examples appear to have been buried intact, leading to the conclusion that the purpose of these ceremonies was not precisely defined and that the Jōmon people imbued these figures with their hopes and prayers in a variety of different ways.

25.
"Snow-goggle" Dogū Figurine

From an archaeological site at Ishinadate,
Rokugō, Misato-chō, Senpoku-gun, Akita Prefecture
Jōmon period, c. 1000–400 B.C.
Earthenware

Height 7 ⅛ inches (18 cm); width 4 ⅝ inches (11.7 cm); depth 2 ½ inches (6.5 cm)
Tokyo National Museum

This figure, known as a "snow-goggle" *dogū*, is one of the best-known types of earthenware figurines in Japan and was common in the northeastern region of the main island of Honshū in the first half of the Final Jōmon period. The name derives from the large, arresting expression of the eyes, which look like the snow goggles worn by the northern peoples, although no research to date has uncovered artifacts from the Jōmon period that resemble such goggles. It is believed instead that the distortion of the facial features, rather than actual goggles, resulted in this exaggerated representation of the eyes.

This figurine is hollow on the inside and admirably demonstrates the superb sense of design, exceptional ability in molding, and proficiency in the earthenware medium evidenced by the Jōmon people. The disproportionately large, preternatural eyes and protruding shoulders and hips with short arms and legs are characteristic features of this figurine. Here, the neck, arms, and ankles are ornamented with a linked-circle design. For the head and the whole of the torso, a technique that combines cord-mark patterned areas with unpatterned areas is used to heighten decorative effect, resulting in a symmetrical decoration of complex, cloudlike patterns.

The prominence of breasts indicates that dogū figurines were intended to be female in gender, and it is believed that the Jōmon people invested them with their prayers and wishes with regard to new life, fertility, and rebirth. **S.Y.**

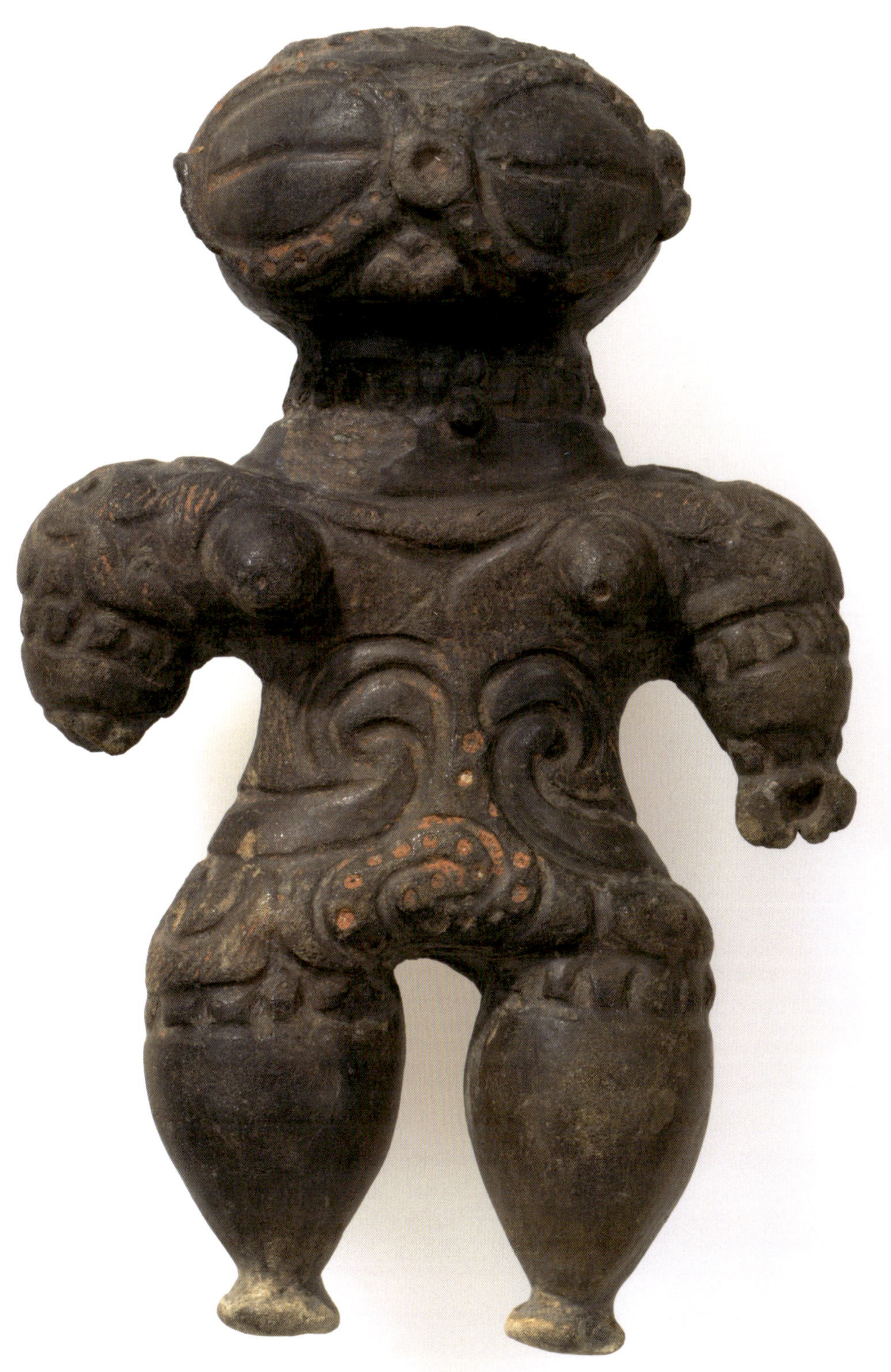

PLATE 25

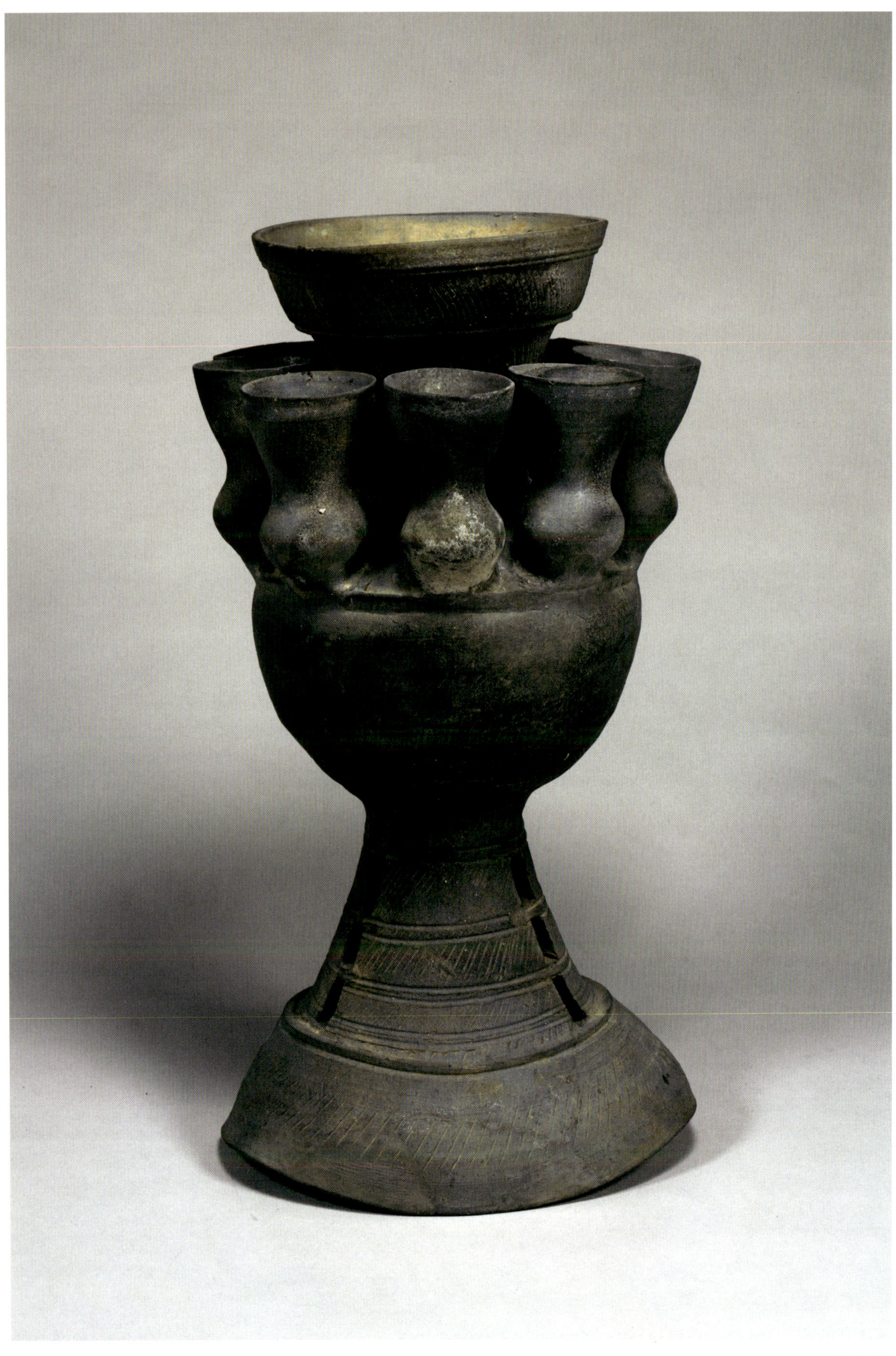

PLATE 26

26.

Jar with Ornaments

From an archaeological site at Maki, Fukuchiyama-shi, Kyoto Prefecture
Late Kofun period, 6th century
Unglazed stoneware, wheel-thrown

Height 16 ⅝ inches (42.2 cm); diameter of mouth 6 ⅞ inches (17.4 cm)
Tokyo National Museum

This piece is composed of a long-necked jar on top of a foot with three tiers of rectangular openwork carvings. The protruding shoulder of the jar is densely lined with eight diminutive long-necked "baby jars," while single and double impressed lines divide the neck and outer surface of the foot into four levels, which are decorated in a design of vertical hatch marks. The jar and stand represented as one form is uniquely found in the Japanese archipelago, and the addition of decorative miniature jars was believed to increase the mystical power of the object. Archaeological findings of this type of artifact have been limited to the interiors of stone chambers or the front of *kofun* tumuli, suggesting that these earthenware vessels must have arisen from a close connection with funeral rites.

Sue wares were earthenware vessels produced in about the first half of the fifth century using new techniques brought to Japan from the Korean Peninsula. Wedged clay was molded using the torque of the potter's wheel, and high-temperature firing in *anagama*-type kilns resulted in a blue-gray, ash-colored ceramic that was very hard in comparison to the reddish-brown, low-temperature-fired Jōmon, Yayoi, and *hajiki* wares. The name *sueki* (Sue ware) is taken from words found in Heian-period documents. Because Sue wares are sensitive to heat, they were used primarily for storage and ceremonial purposes as well as for serving food, rather than for cooking. **F.T.**

In Situ: Buddhist Art and Ritual at the Imperial Court

Melissa McCormick

The highly aestheticized world of Esoteric Buddhist practice and belief, from which many of the objects in this catalogue and related exhibition are drawn, might seem to contradict the common understanding of core Buddhist values, namely the realization of the illusion of the phenomenal world. The gilt-bronze ritual objects included here (Plates 7–11), originally part of large glittering ensembles of implements on altars, the exquisitely decorated sutra (Plate 2) with its frontispiece and its text rendered in alternating lines of gold and silver, or the magnificent fourteenth-century Nirvana painting (Plate 4) executed in sumptuous colors on silk represent an aspect of Buddhist culture that was the opposite of the austerity often associated with the mainstream imagination of Buddhism. Buddhist sutras even include elaborate prescriptive passages for the ornamentation of liturgical settings and illumination of the sutra itself, a kind of sacred adornment (*shōgon*) that became a means of generating karmic merit on behalf of a practitioner or a deceased loved one. The content of the *Golden Light Sutra* (*Konkōmyōkyō*), which played a central role in court Buddhism, not only refers to sacred adornment but also employs language that is itself embellished, using gold metaphorically to describe Buddhas of resplendent brilliance:

> I worship the Buddhas, who are like oceans of virtues, mountains gleaming with the color of gold like Sumeru. I go for refuge to those Buddhas and with my head I bow down to all those Buddhas. [Each one is] gold-colored, shining like pure gold. He has fine eyes, pure and faultless like beryl. He is a mine blazing with glory, splendour, and fame. He is a Buddha-sun removing the obscurity of darkness with his rays of compassion. He is very flawless, very brilliant, with very gleaming limbs. He is a fully enlightened sun. His limbs are as prominent as pure gold.[1]

The concept of shōgon was less rooted in doctrine, however, than in actual ritual practice, and therefore it could manifest in widely divergent ways in terms of objects, materials, craft, and logic of assembly, depending on the region of the Buddhist world in which it appeared. The objects assembled in this catalogue and related exhibition can be understood first and foremost in terms of how shōgon was interpreted by communities of Buddhist practitioners among the Kyoto aristocracy from the eighth to the thirteenth century.

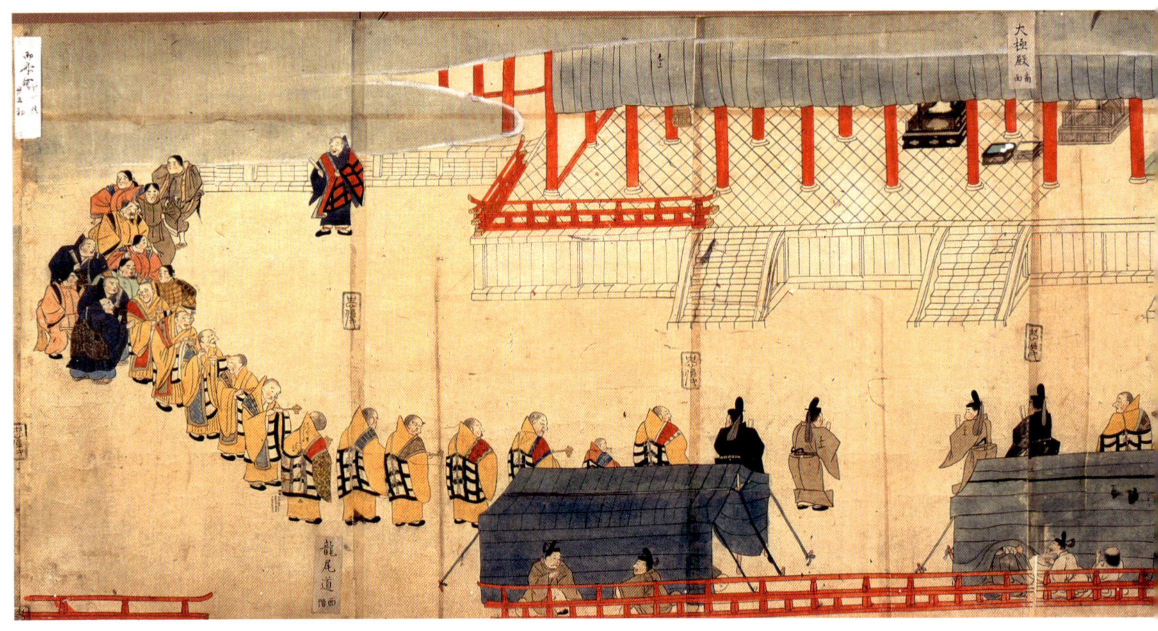

During the Nara (710–94) and Heian periods (794–1185), Buddhist ceremonies figured prominently in court life. A primary example was the so-called Misai-e ceremony depicted in the *Picture Scrolls of the Annual Rites and Ceremonies of the Imperial Court* (*Nenjū gyōji emaki*, fig. 1). This event, the most important religious rite held at court, occurred during the second seven days of the New Year (the 8th through 14th) and consisted of the recitation of and lectures on the *Golden Light Sutra*, quoted previously. The intoning and exposition of this sacred text, said to protect a sovereign and his people from a host of calamities, promised the safety of the realm. In the illustration, court officials followed by the two ritual officiants stand at the head of two lengthy processional lines of priests. Dressed in long ocher robes draped over with surplices (*kesa*), the monks have assembled in the courtyard of the Daigokuden Hall, the palace building within which the sutra recitation will occur. Virtually all of the priests in the procession carry long-handled gilt censers (*egōro*, as seen in Plate 11), reflecting the importance of the smoke of lit incense in Buddhist ritual to demarcate the ritual space, to awaken the senses with an otherworldly perfume, and to link symbolically the dissemination of smoke to that of the Buddha's teachings.[2] The illustration further prompts the viewer to imagine the power of the Misai-e ceremony once all of the monks have been seated inside the hall, their censers releasing the perfumed smoke, and their chanting of the sutra reverberating throughout the palace grounds.

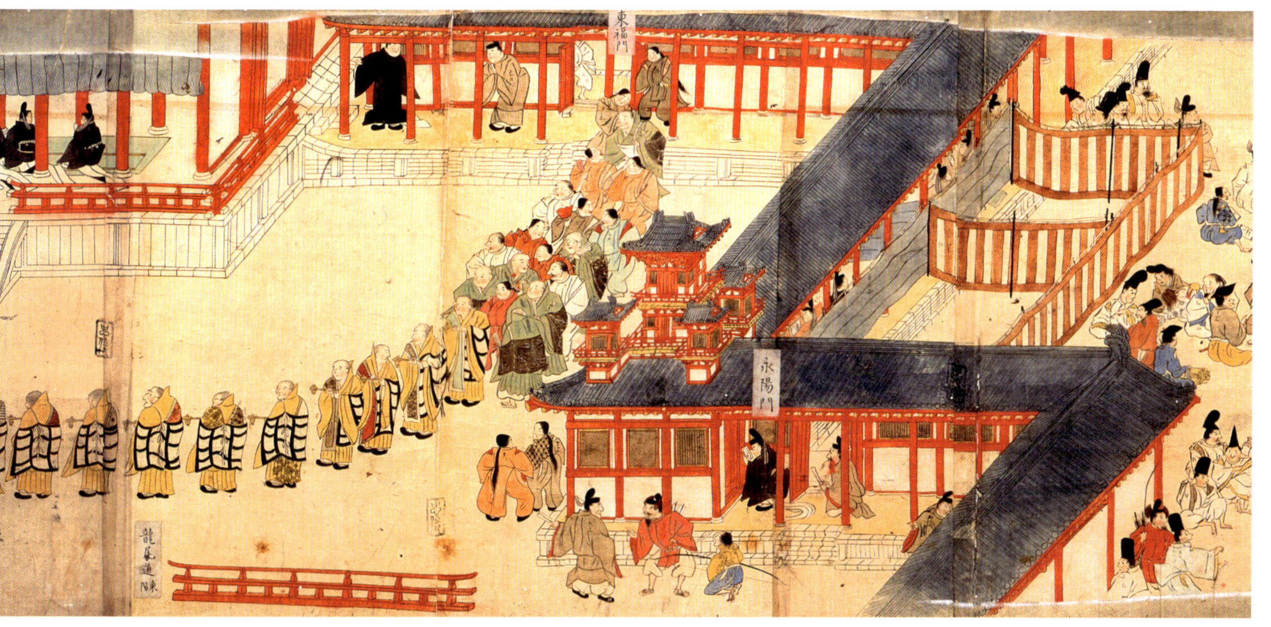

Figure 1
Picture Scrolls of the Annual Rites and Ceremonies of the Imperial Court (Nenjū gyōji emaki), detail of the Misai-e ceremony in the Imperial Palace, painted copy of 12th-century work, dated 1626, by Sumiyoshi Jokei (1599–1670), handscroll, ink, and color on paper, Tanaka Collection.

The arrival of the monk Kūkai in 806, however, altered the dynamic of Buddhist ceremony at the imperial court. Kūkai brought with him the practices of Esoteric Teaching (*mikkyō*) that he had studied during a two-year stay in the Tang capital of Chang'an, and he established the Shingon sect, involving many ritual paradigms and paraphernalia new to Japan, including the use of painted mandalas and large ensembles of gilt-bronze implements. As institutionally vested as the Misai-e rite was, Kūkai managed to persuade the court to expand the New Year Buddhist ceremonies to include a new concurrent Esoteric Buddhist rite called the Mishuhō ceremony.[3] Kūkai argued that the incantation and lecturing of the *Golden Light Sutra* in the existing ceremony was insufficient, and that, for the sutra to be most efficacious, paintings of the deities and altars for their worship had to be built and employed in specifically esoteric rituals. In other words, he made the case for the crucial role of visual images and for an interactive engagement with them in the efficacy of ritual, an argument that would have an indisputably significant impact on the development of Buddhist art in Japan.[4] Kūkai was instrumental in establishing a building dedicated to esoteric ritual within the palace compound known as the Mantra Chapel (Shingon'in), thus securing the presence of Esoteric Buddhist rites physically within the palace and temporally within the calendar of the annual observances of the court.

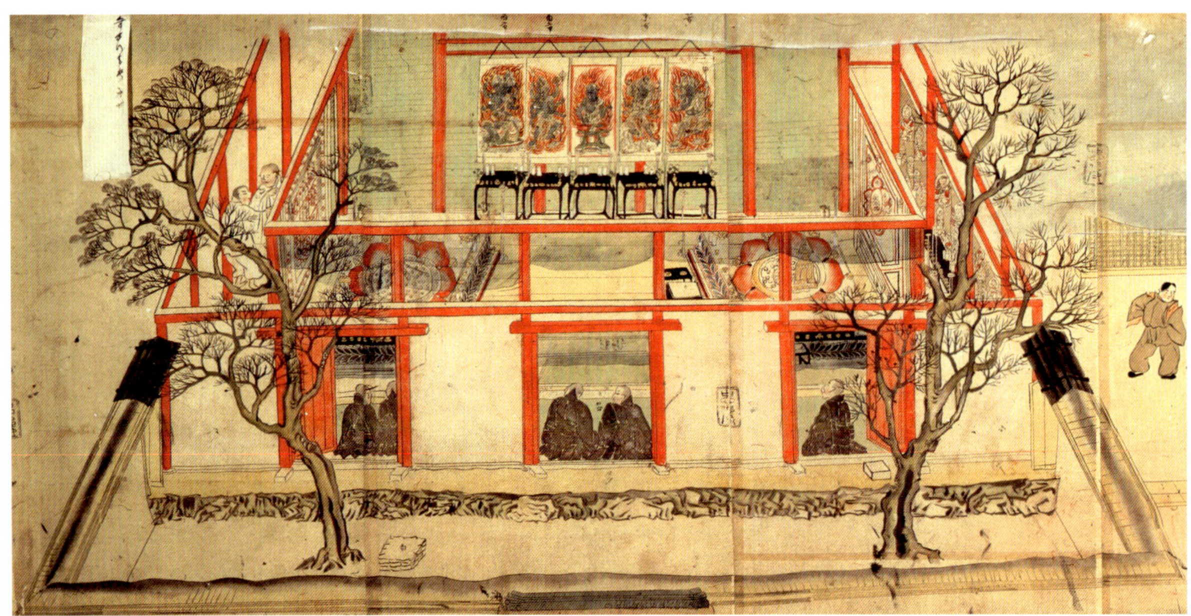

Figure 2
Picture Scrolls of the Annual Rites and Ceremonies of the Imperial Court (Nenjū gyōji emaki), detail of the Mantra Chapel (Shingon'in) in the Imperial Palace, painted copy of 12th-century work, dated 1626, by Sumiyoshi Jokei, handscroll, ink, and color on paper, Tanaka Collection.

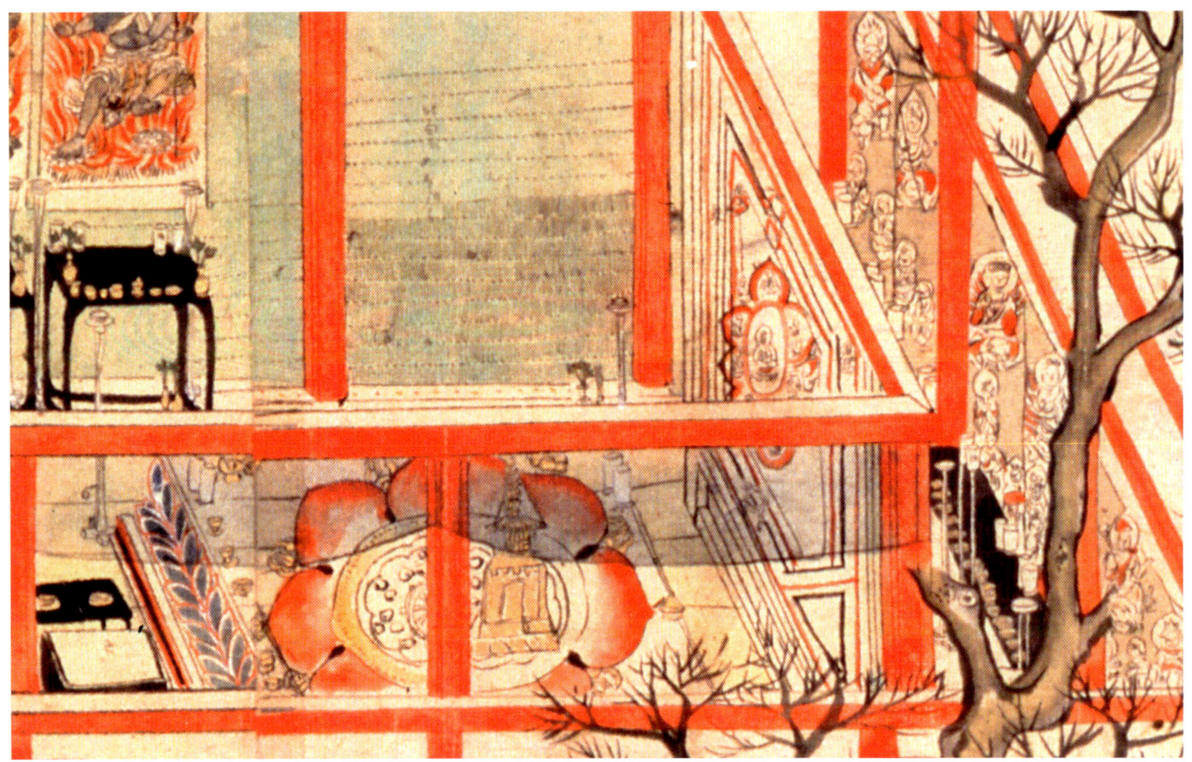

Figure 3
Picture Scrolls of the Annual Rites and Ceremonies of the Imperial Court (Nenjū gyōji emaki), detail of fig. 2, the Mantra Chapel in the Imperial Palace.

Another image from the *Picture Scrolls of the Annual Rites and Ceremonies of the Imperial Court* provides an artistic rendering of the Mantra Chapel, offering an approximation of how more of the objects in this catalogue may have appeared in their original ritual contexts (fig. 2). With the roof of the chapel "removed" in the picture, the viewer may peer down past the three open doors in the seven-bay facade and over and through architectural beams to glimpse the chapel's interior. Hung on the northern wall are separate hanging scrolls of the Five Wrathful Deities (*godai myōō*), also known as the Five Wisdom Kings, fierce emanations and protectors of the Buddhas. Paintings of the Diamond and Womb Realm Mandalas are displayed respectively on the western and eastern walls, while on the ground before them are large and elaborate altars (fig. 3). These great altars would be outfitted with the necessary ritual implements, the offering bowls, incense burner, bell, and five-pronged club, all included in this catalogue.

Although space does not permit an elaboration of the hundreds of ritual actions that occurred within these spaces, the first one to take place during the Mishuhō ceremony, repeated three times a day for seven days, consisted of an offering to Mahāvairocana (known in Japan as Dainichi Nyorai, see Plate 5). This ceremony was performed through ritual and meditative actions by the celebrant and by setting offerings on the great altar before either the Womb Realm Mandala (*taizōkai mandara*) or the Diamond Realm Mandala (*kongōkai mandara*), diagrammatic paintings that attempted to render in visual terms the structure of the Buddhist universe and the cosmic Buddha.[5]

This *Annual Rites and Ceremonies* scroll shows clearly the shallow golden bowls and incense burners lined up around the altar's edge, as well as a miniature stupa placed on top of the lotus-flower pattern that adorns the altar's surface. The miniature stupa used in this ceremony at the court was said to contain grains of a relic of the historical Buddha Śākyamuni and was intricately connected to Kūkai's theoretical basis for the ceremony: the notion that the relic was related to the wish-granting gem in Buddhism, and in turn that the *Golden Light Sutra* itself corresponds to this jewel of the Buddhas. The relic and the stupa could even be incorporated into the details of ritual implements, as in the *Bell with Handle in the Shape of a Stupa* (Plate 10), which may have once contained a relic.

The performative rituals of Esoteric Buddhism engaged all of the observer's senses, and the visually stunning works of art that they featured suited well the aesthetic proclivities of the members of the aristocracy. The theater of Esoteric Buddhism proved to be a welcome vehicle not only for the expression of religious beliefs but also for the demonstration of worldly kingship. Ryūichi Abé has argued that Kūkai's establishment of the Mishuhō rite at the palace was an attempt to "supersede the Confucian characterization of the emperor as the Son of Heaven with that of [the] Buddhist ideal of cakravartin, the universal monarch who pacifies the universe by turning the wheel of the Dharma."[6] The connection between Esoteric Buddhism and the court was thus more than a matter of a shared aesthetic sensibility; the potential for mutually enhancing the authority of the emperor and the

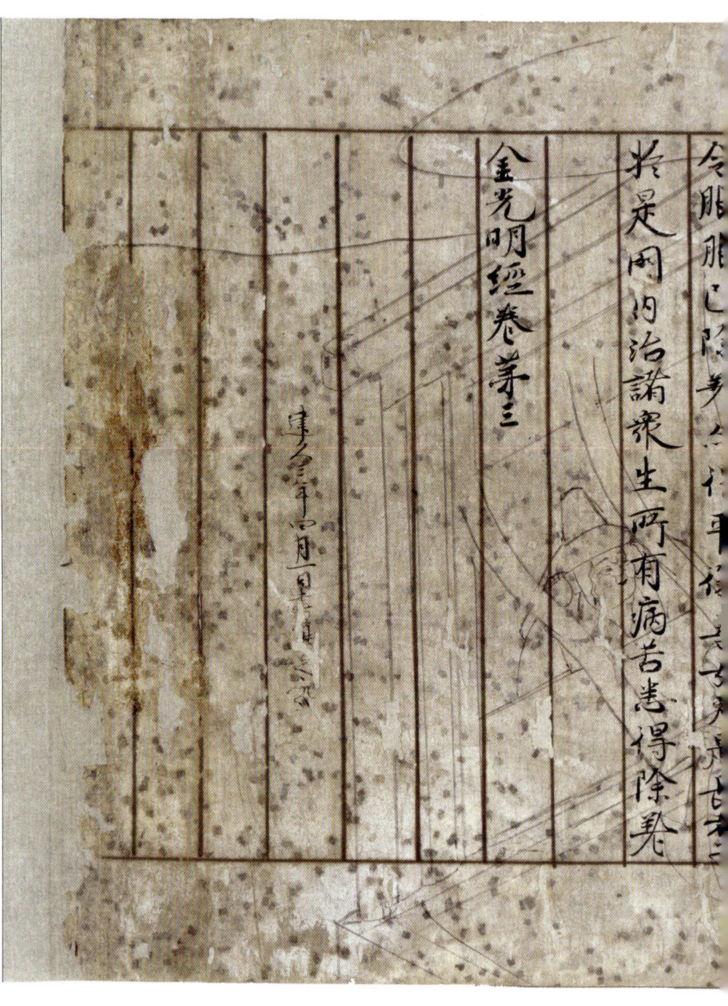

centrality of esoteric practice for the well-being of the country and its ruler was apparent from the beginning. Kūkai's newly established Mishuhō rite involved hundreds of ritual sequences during its seven-day period, but its culmination required the physical presence of the sovereign. Toward the conclusion of the rite, as the officiant chanted, the emperor's robes would be placed on the altar and sprinkled with water. Later he would don those same robes while receiving the sacred water himself.

Whereas the esoteric ritual sited in the imperial court described above, which centered on the *Golden Light Sutra*, involved the body of the sovereign under the pretense of assuring the protection of the nation, court culture embraced Esoteric Buddhism in private ways as well. A perfect embodiment of the personalization of Esotericism and the imperial house is a copy of the *Golden Light Sutra*, with its characters superimposed over underdrawings, which was created after the death of Emperor Goshirakawa in 1192 as a dedicatory offering. The images in these underdrawings, which depict women with long hair and round faces wearing multilayered robes and seated within architectural settings seen from a bird's-eye-view perspective, resemble the illustrations of a narrative tale. These pictures are unfinished, however, lacking the rich pigments and final touches of black ink that typically articulate facial features in Heian-period picture scrolls. Peeking out from beneath the sutra script are the eyeless figures that give the work its nickname, the "eyeless sutra" (*Menashikyō*) (fig. 4). A postscript to another sutra in the set reveals that the underdrawings, as personal possessions of the deceased emperor or drawings executed in his own hand, constituted the appropriate paper ground for the sacred text when the emperor passed away before their completion.[7] When considering the meaning of the central role of the *Golden Light Sutra* in court ceremony, the "eyeless sutra" may be interpreted as another example of the fusion of imperial identity, court culture, and Esoteric Buddhist practice.

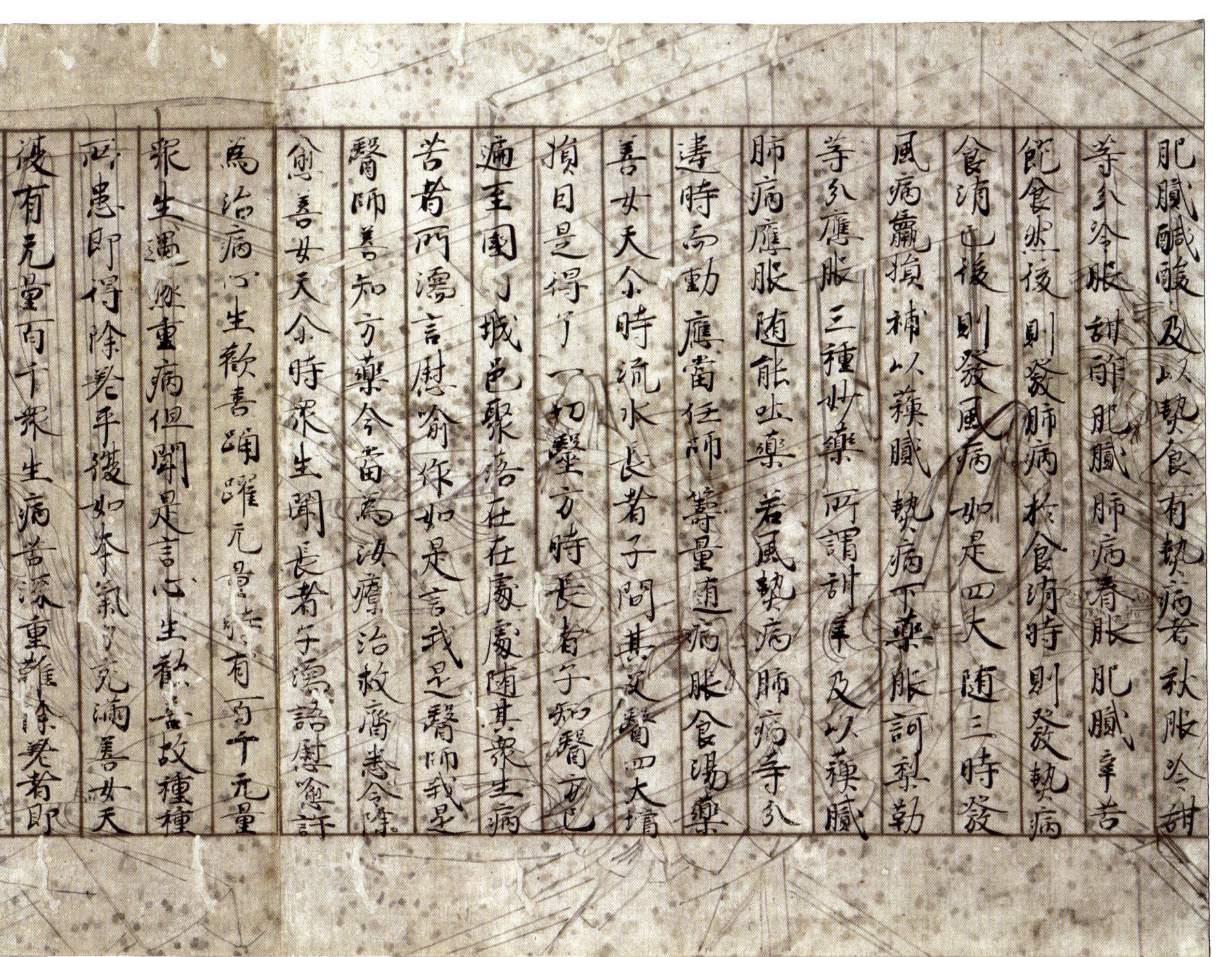

Figure 4
Golden Light Sutra (*Konkōmyōkyō*), with underdrawings, known as the "eyeless sutra" (*Menashikyō*), 12th century, ink on paper, Kyoto National Museum.

With the diminution of imperial power during the Kamakura period and beyond into the Warring States period, lavish court rituals became a thing of the past. After the reunification of the country under the Tokugawa rulers in the seventeenth century, however, a number of court ceremonies were reinstituted, including the Mishuhō in 1623,[8] during the reign of Emperor Gomizunoo (1596–1680; r. 1611–29), son of Emperor Goyōzei (r. 1586–1611), whose calligraphy is represented in this catalogue (Plate 3). Although it might be tempting to interpret the reestablishment of spectacular Esoteric Buddhist rites at the palace as a courtly revival, the ceremonies took place under the watchful eye of the Tokugawa shogunate. The military rulers had strategically arranged a marriage between Gomizunoo and Tōfukumon'in, daughter of the second Tokugawa shogun, Hidetada, giving them direct access to the throne. The grand scale on which Gomizunoo and his Tokugawa consort patronized Buddhist institutions and revitalized Buddhist ritual at the court must therefore be understood within the context of Tokugawa control of the imperial institution. In such a context of Tokugawa hegemony, an aggrandizement of the sovereign vis-à-vis Buddhist ritual could only benefit the military rulers, who could boast of controlling not merely the sovereign, but also the universal monarch and ultimately Buddhist power itself. The courtly aesthetic linking Esoteric Buddhism and ritual thus lived on, but in a strikingly different form than Kūkai could have envisioned in the tenth century.

Notes

1. *The Sūtra of Golden Light: Being a Translation of the Suvarṇabhāsottamasūtra*, 3rd rev. ed., trans. R. E. Emmerick (Oxford: Pali Text Society, 2001), 13–14.

2. Anne Nishimura Morse and Samuel Crowell Morse explain the important relationship between transcendent religious experience and the aesthetic in Japanese Buddhist art, specifically the meaning and ritual function of implements, such as the censer, in *Object as Insight: Japanese Buddhist Art and Ritual* (Katonah NY: Katonah Museum of Art, 1995), see esp. 67, 126–27.

3. Ryūichi Abé, *The Weaving of Mantra: Kūkai and the Construction of Esoteric Buddhist Discourse* (New York: Columbia University Press, 1999), 344–55, discusses in detail the various esoteric rites that took place within the palace grounds.

4. The centrality of the visual to Esoteric Buddhism, its precedents, and its implications are thoroughly discussed in Cynthea J. Bogel, *With a Single Glance: Buddhist Icon and Early Mikkyō Vision* (Seattle: University of Washington Press, 2009).

5. For more on mandalas in Esoteric Buddhist practice, see Elizabeth ten Grotenhuis, *Japanese Mandalas: Representations of Sacred Geography* (Honolulu: University of Hawaii Press, 1999).

6. Abé, *The Weaving of Mantra*, 65.

7. Willa J. Tanabe, *Paintings of the Lotus Sutra* (New York: Weatherhill, 1988), 59–60; for the Japanese inscription see Nara Kokuritsu Hakubustukan, ed., *Tokubetsuten josei to bukkyō: inori to hohoemi* (Nara: Nara National Museum, 2003), 222.

8. Abé, *The Weaving of Mantra*, 347.

Checklist of the Exhibition

Plate 1
Man'yōshū, Vol. 9 (Takamatsunomiya version)
National Treasure
Heian period, 11th century
One of a set of twenty bound booklets, ink on paper
9 ¾ x 6 ¾ inches (25 x 17 cm)
Tokyo National Museum

Plate 2
Daitō Saiiki ki (Record of the Chinese Priest Xuanzang's Journey to the West), Vol. 1
Important Cultural Property
Heian period, 12th century
One of a set of twelve handscrolls, gold and silver on indigo paper
With mounting: 10 ⅛–10 ⅜ inches (25.6–26.3 cm) x 251 ¾–569 ⅝ inches (639.3–1446.9 cm);
Without mounting: 10 x 424 ⅜ inches (25.3 x 1078.1 cm)
Tokyo National Museum

Plate 3
Characters "Dragon" and "Tiger"
By Emperor Goyōzei (1571–1617)
Important Art Object
Azuchi-Momoyama period, 16th–17th century
Hanging scroll, ink on decorative paper
47 ⅝ x 21 inches (120.8 x 53.3 cm)
Tokyo National Museum

Plate 4
Nirvana Painting
Kamakura period, 14th century
Hanging scroll, color on silk
75 ⅛ x 47 ⅜ inches (190.7 x 120.4 cm)
Tokyo National Museum

Plate 5
Seated Dainichi Nyorai
Important Cultural Property
Heian period, 11th century
Lacquered wood with gold leaf
Height of figure 36 ¾ inches (93.4 cm); height of pedestal 24 ⅛ inches (61.2 cm)
Tokyo National Museum

Plate 6
Standing Zaō Gongen
Kamakura period, 12th–13th century
Bronze
Height: 11 ¼ inches (28.5 cm)
Tokyo National Museum

Plate 7
Kasha (Incense Burner) and Set of Six Ritual Bowls
Kamakura period, 13th–14th century
Gilt bronze
Kasha: height 4 ⅝ inches (11.7 cm);
burner: height 2 ⅛ inches (5.4 cm), diameter 4 ¾ inches (11.9 cm), height of lid 2 ⅝ inches (6.5 cm), diameter of lid 4 ½ inches (11.4 cm);
six ritual bowls: height 1 ¾ inches (4.2 cm), diameter of mouth 3 ⅛–3 ¼ inches (8–8.1 cm), height of base 1 ⅝ inches (4.1 cm), height of bowls ⅞ inch (2.2–2.3 cm),
diameter of bowls 3–3 ⅛ inches (7.6–7.8 cm), height of bowl bases ⅝–⅞ inches (1.6–1.8 cm), diameter of bowl bases 2 ⅛–2 ⅜ inches (5.4–6.1 cm)
Tokyo National Museum

Plate 8
Five-pronged Vajra Bell
Heian period, 12th century
Gilt bronze
Height 6 ½ inches (16.6 cm);
diameter of mouth 2 ⅞ inches (7.4 cm)
Tokyo National Museum

Plate 9
Five-pronged Vajra Club
Kamakura period, 13th century
Gilt bronze
Length 7 inches (17.9 cm)
Tokyo National Museum

Plate 10
Bell with Handle in the Shape of a Stupa
Kamakura period, 13th century
Gilt bronze
Height 6 ½ inches (21 cm);
diameter of mouth 2 ⅞ inches (8 cm)
Tokyo National Museum

Plate 11
Incense Burner with Handle
Heian period, 12th century
Gilt bronze
Length 14 ⅛ inches (35.8 cm);
diameter of burner cup 4 ¼ inches (10.6 cm)
Tokyo National Museum

Plate 12
Shō (mouth-organ) called "Mura-chidori"
By Sono Hironaga
Edo period, dated 1690
Bamboo and lacquered wood with maki-e
sprinkled gold design bearing inscriptions
identifying artist and date
Length 18 inches (45.8 cm)
Tokyo National Museum

Plate 13
Ryūteki (dragon flute) called "Ashitazu"
Muromachi period, 15th century
Bamboo wrapped with black
lacquered bark strips
Length 15 ¾ inches (40 cm)
Tokyo National Museum

Plate 14
Hichiriki (flageolet-like instrument) called "Higurashi"
Kamakura period, 13th century
Bamboo wrapped with black
lacquered bark strips
Length 7 ¼ inches (18.2 cm)
Tokyo National Museum

Plate 15
Square Dish with Autumn Grasses Design
Nezumi-Shino type, Mino ware
Azuchi-Momoyama to Edo period, 16th–17th century
Glazed stoneware
7 ½ x 9 ⅞ inches (19 cm x 22.5 cm),
height 1 ¾ inches (4.5 cm)
Tokyo National Museum

Plate 16
Tea Bowl
Hori (carved) Karatsu type, Karatsu ware
Azuchi-Momoyama to Edo period, 16th–17th century
Glazed stoneware
Height 3 ⅞ inches (9.9 cm);
diameter of mouth 4 ½–4 ¾ inches (11.5–12 cm);
diameter of bottom 3 ⅜ inches (8.7 cm)
Gift of Mr. Hirota Matsushige
Tokyo National Museum

Plate 17
Water Jar with Handles
Iga ware
Edo period, 17th century
Natural ash-glazed stoneware
Height 7 ¾ inches (19.5 cm);
diameter of mouth 5 ⅞ inches (14.9 cm)
Tokyo National Museum

Plate 18
Flower Vase with Square Mouth
Iga ware
Edo period, 17th century
Natural ash-glazed stoneware
Height 6 ⅝ inches (16.8 cm);
diameter of mouth 4 ¾ inches (12.3 cm);
diameter of bottom 4 ¼ inches (11 cm)
Tokyo National Museum

Plate 19
Pail-shaped Sake Cask with Design of Pine and Bamboo
Kyoto ware
Edo period, 18th century
Glazed stoneware with overglaze enamels
Height 7 ¾ inches (19.6 cm);
diameter 5 inches (12.6 cm);
diameter of bottom 3 ⅛ inches (7.8 cm)
Tokyo National Museum

Plate 20
Tenmoku Tea Bowl with Interlocking Circle Design
Kyoto ware, with mark "Iwakurayama"
Edo period, 18th century
Glazed stoneware with overglaze enamels
Height 2 ½ inches (6.3 cm);
diameter of mouth 4 ¼ inches (10.9 cm);
diameter of bottom 1 ⅝ inches (4.1 cm)
Tokyo National Museum

Plate 21
Dish with Design of Dandelions
Nabeshima ware
Edo period, 18th century
Glazed porcelain with overglaze enamels
Height 2 ⅛ inches (5.4 cm);
diameter 8 inches (20.2 cm);
diameter of foot 4 ¼ inches (10.8 cm)
Tokyo National Museum

Plate 22
Chrysanthemum-shaped Bowl with
Design of Chrysanthemums
Imari ware
Edo period, 18th century
Glazed porcelain with overglaze enamels
Height 3 inches (7.5 cm);
diameter of mouth 9 inches (22.8 cm);
diameter of foot 5 inches (12.8 cm)
Tokyo National Museum

Plate 23
Four-lobed Bowl with Design of Cherry
Blossoms and Maple Trees
By Takahashi Dōhachi II (Ninnami Dōhachi,
1783–1855), with mark "Dōhachi"
Edo period, 19th century
Glazed stoneware with overglaze enamels
Height 3 ½ inches (8.8 cm);
diameter of mouth 6 ½ inches (16.5 cm);
diameter of bottom 3 ⅛ inches (7.9 cm)
Tokyo National Museum

Plate 24
Square Dish with Design of Young
Pines and Distant Mountains
By Eiraku Wazen (1823–1896)
Edo–Meiji period, 19th century
Glazed porcelain with overglaze enamels
1 ½ x 8 ½ x 8 ¼ inches (3.7 x 21.5 x 20.9 cm)
Tokyo National Museum

Plate 25
"Snow-goggle" Dogū Figurine
From an archaeological site at Ishinadate, Rokugō,
Misato-chō, Senpoku-gun, Akita Prefecture
Jōmon period, c. 1000–400 B.C.
Earthenware
Height 7 ⅛ inches (18 cm);
width 4 ⅝ inches (11.7 cm);
depth 2 ½ inches (6.5 cm)
Tokyo National Museum

Plate 26
Jar with Ornaments
Sue ware
From an archaeological site at Maki,
Fukuchiyama-shi, Kyoto Prefecture
Late Kofun period, 6th century
Unglazed stoneware, wheel-thrown
Height 16 ⅝ inches (42.2 cm);
diameter of mouth 6 ⅞ inches (17.4 cm)
Tokyo National Museum